BRIGADIER GENERAL ROBERT HIPWELL

# INSPIRATIONAL LEADERSHIP

Stories of Valor from an American Hero to Educate, Empower, and Inspire You and Your Team

Publishing Process by www.PlugAndPlayPublishing.com

Book Cover by Tracey Miller | www.TraceOfStyle.com

Book Written by Robert Hipwell and Dan Janal.

Book Edited by Jenny Butterfield Lyon

ISBN: 9798363761959



Conversations in this book have been reconstructed and edited for clarity.

To my wife, Cindy.

Cindy is my rock. She is my confidant. We've been married for over 30 years, and I wouldn't be the person I am today without her love for me, her love for our family, her rugged determination, her quest for perfection, and her passion for life. She's everything to me in the world. Cindy is the best thing that ever happened to me.

# Praise for Bob Hipwell and "Inspirational Leadership"

"Brigadier General (Ret.) Bob Hipwell stood out as a leader during the Surge in Iraq and in numerous other assignments, and *Inspirational Leadership* conveys why that was the case, capturing the essence of the dynamic leadership he provided. General Hipwell explains superbly the critical importance of a leader providing energy, example, competence, drive, and sincere compassion for those in the leader's charge. And he shares wonderful vignettes from his storied career to illustrate powerfully the points he makes. *Inspirational Leadership* is a wonderful book by a great soldier and leader!"

-**General David Petraeus**, Former Commander of the Surge in Iraq, U.S. Central Command, and NATO/U.S. Forces in Afghanistan, and former Director of the CIA

"If you want to lead your team through action, then follow Brigadier General (Ret) Robert Hipwell's principles for inspirational leadership success!"

-**General JD Thurman**, Former Commander of United Nations Command, R.O.K.-U.S. Combined Forces Command, and United States Forces Korea and the former Chief, Operations, Coalition Forces Land Component Command (CFLCC), Operation Iraqi Freedom

"*Inspirational Leadership* is a firsthand account of life and death experiences, and how to persevere when the going gets tough. This gripping book is filled with personal stories during both peace and wartime of leadership and inspiration. This book will elevate thinking about devotion and commitment. I highly recommend this book to leaders who want to find new ways to make a difference."

**-Mary Kelly**, Commander, USN, CSP, CPAE, Author of *Who Comes Next? Leadership Succession Made Easy*

"A lifetime of commitment, integrity, and honor shines in this very personal take on principles of leadership. Robert Hipwell has experienced combat from the triple-canopy jungle of Vietnam to the desert plains of Iraq, from green recruit to Brigadier General, from the '60s through 2010. His personal journey has taken him from middle-class San Diego through blue-collar England to Ph.D. scholarship and many civilian leadership roles; a man with common roots in an uncommon search for honor and excellence emerges. A rewarding read from any viewpoint!"

**-Hank Walther**, MD

"I see Robert as somebody who has led an extraordinary life and likely has some incredible lessons to teach us."

**-Doug Greene**, WhatReallyMattersInterviews.com podcast

"I had the privilege of serving as General Hipwell's Sergeant Major during 07-08 in Iraq. His dedication to his troops and mission earned him the respect of those he commanded. General Hipwell's military career speaks volumes of honorable service to our nation over the decades. I highly recommend his writings which can be lessons in leadership, values, and commitment, of putting the welfare of our nation and people ahead of our own."

**-Richard Winkleman**, Sergeant Major,
United States, Retired

"Unique and highly engaging. As a former Task Force Agent with the FBI, I can appreciate the life Bob Hipwell has lived as he personifies Duty, Honor, Country. Very few of our nation's soldiers have served as long and with such distinction from an NCO Ranger/ Special Forces soldier in Vietnam to the battles General Hipwell led in Iraq. His book on leadership uses his unique experiences to offer up a breadth of unforgettable real-world lessons for anyone seeking to improve their leadership skills. This is a must-read for any institution."

**-WC Ballinger**

"I was truly inspired by the book written by General Robert Hipwell. As a retired veteran of 32 years in the Air Force and Coast Guard and a Vietnam Veteran, I experienced some of the same scenarios that General Hipwell experienced, except for hanging upside down from a helicopter. I started reading his life story and I could not stop reading it until the conclusion. It was thought-provoking and he made all his experiences come back to life. What an incredible life and family story. I highly recommend his book to civilians and military members. You will not be disappointed. I am reading it again because of its true-to-life story."

**-Gary Johnson**, Brigadier General USV-A, Air Force and Coast Guard (Retired), National Board Member VAREP

# Table of Contents

# Foreword
# The Army Values

This book is based on some of the best, time-tested values you'll find anywhere: The Army Values.

I've lived by these values while serving in the U.S. Army, U.S. Army Reserve, and the National Guard, as well as in my business, professional, and personal lives. I share these values with you so that you can begin to live your life based on these time-honored and proven principles.

Below is the basic overview from the Army's website. However, in each chapter, I will detail how the Army defines these values and how I inspired and led my teams (up to 10,000 troops) as well as my blended family, including nine children and 24 grandkids.

Here are the Army values, as introduced on the Army website (https://www.army.mil/values):

> Many people know what the words Loyalty, Duty, Respect, Selfless Service, Honor, Integrity, and Personal Courage mean. But how often do you see someone live

> up to them? Soldiers learn these values in detail beginning during Basic Combat Training (BCT); from then on, they live them every day in everything they do—whether they're on the job or off. In short, the Seven Core Army Values listed below are what being a professional Soldier is all about.

I hope these values inspire you to accomplish your goals and lead your teams to the next level and beyond.

# Overview

Millions of American men and women have voluntarily joined the armed forces since that fateful day on September 11, 2001—9/11—when the world changed forever.

These soldiers served their country and returned to a hero's welcome—and a workplace that didn't quite understand them.

These patriots lived by core values. In the Army, those values are loyalty, duty, respect, selfless service, honor, integrity, and personal courage.

Those values molded these people in ways that civilians have never been exposed to. These soldiers didn't merely hear those principles; they lived those principles.

They brought back invaluable skills to help companies improve teamwork, leadership, the ability to think on their feet, and the facility to respond to crises and threats. Those actionable skills are gifts that veterans can give to companies.

However, these heroes also brought back their battle scars. Some injuries you can see, such as missing limbs and prosthetics. Some injuries you can't see: PTSD, TMI (traumatic brain injury), and survivor's guilt (when a person feels guilty because they survived a life-threatening event that others did not).

These soldiers can become some of the most productive workers and leaders you will ever hire.

My mission for this book is three-fold:

1. Show companies they can profit from hiring veterans who will be their ideal workers.
2. Help returning veterans enter a multitude of workplaces that are eager to hire them and use their unique talents, skills, and abilities.
3. Make America a stronger country as a result of this partnership.

Highlighting real-life adventures as well as questions for education, information, and inspiration, my goal is to help readers understand the veteran's mindset so leaders and veterans can create effective teams, productive workplaces, and inspiring atmospheres.

I hope this easy-to-read book will give leaders insight into the terrific people they will hire from the military. The stories and lessons will provide sound and practical advice for creating empowering workplaces.

## My Story

As a soldier at the ripe old age of 19, I deployed to South Vietnam to begin my tour of duty.

As part of a Long-Range Recognizance Patrol (LRRP) Company, I was assigned to a six-man team. We conducted long-range reconnaissance patrols.

We were inserted into the triple canopy jungle, airlifted deep into the Central Highlands by Huey helicopters, and escorted by Cobra Gun Ships. The Huey's flew us about 50-100 miles west of our firebase (Camp Eagle, home of the 101st Airborne Division in RVN) and landed in what I called "the belly of the beast to report back daily to higher HQs what the beast was eating."

**Photo was taken in April 1970, when the author was 19 years old (19 years was the average age of a soldier serving in Vietnam), while serving his tour of duty with Company L (Ranger) 75th Infantry at Camp Eagle, Republic of Vietnam.**

We looked down on the Ho Chi Minh Trail as the North Vietnamese Army (NVA) passed through our area of interest/focus known as the "A Shau Valley." We watched to see what the enemy was doing. Our Standard Operating Procedure (SOP) was to radio back to higher HQs using a SALUTE Report (Size, Activity, Location, Unit, Time, and Equipment). We observed them and could smell what they were eating. We observed what their trucks carried. We saw and reported how many NVA were in their patrols.

Most of our LRRP missions were about five days out in the bush. The Army would insert our six-man LRRP Team into a hilltop (usually a burned-out old firebase) for a five-day recon mission (Monday through Friday), and extract (airlift) us back to our firebase for the weekends. We did this over and over again. That was our job.

They usually would airlift in Huey helicopters three to five LRRP teams early in the morning onto different hilltops close to each other. In early May 1970, my LRRP Team was inserted into a jungle hilltop on my second or third mission, and another team was inserted into a nearby hilltop (about 5 kilometers away). Soon after the other team was inserted, a fierce firefight erupted, and all six soldiers were killed in action (KIA). They never made it back alive. My team didn't get engaged on that particular mission. We did our recon job, and all six of us came back to the safety of our firebase.

When I got back to the safety of our firebase, I reflected, "Wow, they could have put my LRRP Team down on that hot LZ (hilltop) and put the other team down on our landing zone (LZ), then my team and I would be all KIA."

I've always tried to live my life in an honorable way because those soldiers never returned. Their average age was just 20 years old. They died way too young and never had the opportunity to mature, get married, and have families. Their parents were denied grandkids.

When I enjoy all the holidays and fun things that happen in my life with my family and friends, I think back to that day. I remind myself that life should be lived with zest and appreciation for all those who fought to allow us to enjoy our American way of life. I've tried to build my life in a way that I would honor, respect, and never forget those young men's ultimate sacrifice. Everybody in our military family has sacrificed their time, talents, and sometimes their lives to allow all of us to live the American dream of pursuing our happiness and living long, strong, and prosperously.

Do you want to be remembered as the person who lives up to these principles?

Are you helping to make/shape the people around you better? Are you helping your company?

Are you helping fulfill your dreams and your missions?

My driving force in life is to educate, empower, and inspire people to take ownership of their own lives and move forward in the direction they want to move in and live a purpose-filled life.

You've probably heard this old story. There are two wolves inside each person: the good wolf and a bad wolf. If you feed the bad wolf, that's the person you're going to be. But if you feed the good wolf and move forward, you will have more positive things happen in your world and the world around you.

I belong to a couple of websites that offer positive affirmations and stories. I also listen to positive self-hypnosis programs when our minds are most receptive to inputs. These critically receptive times are just before going to sleep, for about half an hour after going into REM sleep, and when you first wake up. I get pinged every day with positive, inspirational messages that help keep my thoughts more positive. I hang out with and follow good, inspirational people. I'm trying to feed the good wolf versus the bad wolf, so I won't go down the path I don't want to be on.

When I speak to veteran's groups, I remind them of the movie, *Saving Private Ryan*. There's a small but subtle caveat at the very end, which most people don't pick up on if they've only seen the movie once. But I've seen that movie 25 times or so. Captain Miller is sitting on the bridge. He's wounded. He's dying. He's bleeding out, leaning up against that old Ural motorcycle. And he motions for Private Ryan to get closer so he can say something to him.

Ryan goes over to him.

Captain Miller whispers in his ear, "Earn this. Earn it!"

What does that mean?

It means that Miller and eight other Rangers sacrificed their lives for Ryan so that he could return home safely.

Millions of other Americans have been fighting for our freedoms. They have put their lives on the line, and many died so that we can continue to live the American Dream. They've given all their tomorrows for us so that we could enjoy a tomorrow and live a good life.

At the end of the movie, this idea hits home when an older Private Ryan and his family are in France visiting the Normandy American Cemetery, which contains the graves of over 9,000 of our military dead, most of whom lost their lives in the D-Day landings. After he sees Captain Miller's tombstone, Ryan asks his wife, "Have I lived a good life?"

She says, "Of course you have."

He was trying to live up to what Captain John Miller told him on the bridge.

If I could have some little caveat like that, I would want people to say, "Hey, I want to live a good life, contribute to my community and society, and help people move forward. That's what I would like to do."

Every time I see that movie, that message hits me deep inside because I think of the six young men on that hill in Vietnam, all of whom were KIA. It could easily have been me but for divine intervention, luck, or karma. I want to live a good life. And I want you to be inspired to live a good life, share some of my stories, and inspire, educate, and empower future leaders with this book.

## About Robert (Bob) Hipwell

I'm the son of an immigrant family. My father, Harry, and mother, Mary, were born in Liverpool, England. So was I and my sweet sister, Susan. We all came to settle in California via Canada, where for seven years, my father worked building ships at a Canadian Shipyard near Victoria.

For the next seven years, we lived in Victoria, where my lovely sister, Laverne, and hockey-playing, surfing, and triathlete brother, Martin, were born.

Our final family move was to San Diego, where my dad moved up in the shipbuilding world and got a better job as a foreman. Our family was finally complete when my younger, soccer-playing brothers, Paul and Peter, were born.

Now you could say we were a complete family, which included Peter, Paul, Mary, Laverne, Susan, Harry, Robert, Martin, and Barry. Barry was a high school friend who moved in with us because his family situation was not very stable.

I attended high school in San Diego, and I was on the swim team and played saxophone in the Kearny High School marching band. I graduated from high school in June 1968, at the height of the Vietnam War. Most people know San Diego as a classy city that loves and supports all our military service members.

My high school buddy (Danny) and I saw the movie, *The Green Berets,* starring John Wayne. That movie took me over the edge. As soon as we graduated high school, I anticipated getting drafted so I signed up for three years. Danny and I joined the Army on the "Buddy System." Eventually, we both served in Vietnam, and both of us became Airborne, Rangers, and Green Berets.

I wanted to be a paratrooper. I had watched many movies on TV with my Dad about World War II, Paratroopers, the 82nd Airborne Division, and the 101st Airborne Division. I was privileged and honored to later serve with L Company 75th Infantry (Ranger), 101st Airborne Division, at Camp Eagle in the Republic of South Vietnam (RVN).

During the time of the Vietnam War, the US had over 500,000 troops deployed to South Vietnam.

At the height of the Vietnam war, starting with the Tet Offensive and during 1968, the U.S. suffered almost 17,000 KIAs (killed in action) and over 87,000 WIAs (wounded in action). Because the Army "leads from the front," there was a high cost in the lives of our Non-Commissioned Officers (NCOs), first sergeants, and lieutenants.

I joined the Army when they were in dire need of fresh troops and junior leaders. So, I was moved into the fast lane. The Army set up leadership academies (for NCOs and Officers) to quickly promote soldiers to sergeant and lieutenant. I went on a fast track and became a sergeant seven months after entering the Army at the ripe old age of 18.

Within seven months of volunteering for the Army, I had completed basic training (BCT), advanced individual training (AIT), and an NCO Academy. I was promoted to Sergeant.

About 90% of my graduating class from the NCO Academy received orders for immediate duty in Vietnam. I had Airborne training on my contract, so just before the end of NCO Academy, the Army Ranger recruiters came to our training company area looking for Ranger School candidates. Danny and I were qualified, and we both volunteered to attend Ranger School, one of the toughest training schools in the Army.

Ranger School is 61 days of spartan-type training (24/7) focused on leadership and small unit tactics with very little time for sleep and long periods of food deprivation. After graduating from Ranger School, we also got our opportunity to attend Airborne Training at Fort Benning, Georgia. I have fond memories of Airborne training during July of 1969 and watching Neil Armstrong become the first man to walk on the moon. My fellow Airborne Trainees and I watched this historic event on a small black and white TV with aluminum foil on the bunny ears from the Day Room. Before we checked out of Airborne School, Danny and I received orders for duty in Vietnam and soon afterward reported to Fort Lewis, Washington, for immediate deployment to the Republic of Vietnam (RVN).

However, the day we were to ship overseas, President Nixon ordered a pause in Troop deployments. He said that for now, no more troops were being sent to RVN. I was sent to Fort Hood, Texas. I was assigned to the 5/6 Mech Infantry Battalion, 1st Armored Division.

Soon after I arrived, I was selected for and completed Recondo Training (short for Reconnaissance Commando). Soon afterward, my mechanized infantry company was chosen for a short NATO Tour in England. After we returned from England, in early April 1970, my unit was tasked with sending filler troops to RVN. I came down on a levy and soon received another set of orders for duty in RVN.

Upon arrival in RVN in early April 1970, I reported to the in-country processing center. Since I was Ranger qualified, they asked if I wanted to be assigned to a Ranger Company and I said, "okay." I was assigned to L Company 75th Infantry

(Ranger) and did a tour as a long-range reconnaissance (LRRP) assistant patrol leader. As LRRPs, our primary mission was to monitor the enemy along the A Shau Valley in the sector of the combat zone known as the Ho Chi Minh Trail and report on their activities. More about that later.

After almost three years of active service (the Army was drawing down and released many soldiers early), I returned to San Diego and got a construction job in the shipyard where my dad worked. The shipyard completed its last big contract of building 17 Navy LST ships for the Navy, and then they began laying off workers. After six months, I got laid off. With no job prospects on the horizon, I decided to go to England with my British-born wife.

We went to Hull in northeastern England for three years. I attended night school classes with the help of the Montgomery GI Bill. I received an "O" level certificate in physics and mathematics. While living in England, I stayed active in Army Reserve and did a couple of annual training tours in Germany.

Three years later, when I came back to San Diego, I joined the California National Guard and was selected to attend an officer training program, State Officer Candidate School (OCS).

Two years after that, I was honored to be commissioned a second lieutenant. Soon after that, I switched from the Army National Guard to the Army Reserve and was assigned to the

2nd Battalion, 12th Special Forces Group (U.S. Army Green Berets).

In 1983, I was promoted to captain. I had completed the special forces officer's qualification course (SFOQC) by then. I was honored to serve as an Operational Detachment A (ODA) Team Commander (a 12-man ODA team) and deployed overseas on many missions (mainly to South Korea) during the "Cold War Period."

Fast forward from there, and during the last ten years of my 42 years in uniform, I became an Army Military Police Officer. I had the good fortune to work with great people and inspirational mentors. I got promoted to Brigadier General and was also selected to command an MP Brigade, stationed in Inkster, Michigan. On my promotion packet, I checked the box that said, "If selected, I will serve at the needs of the Army and be assigned to a unit outside a 50-mile radius of my home of record (HOR)." As a drilling reservist living in California, I flew to Michigan to attend reserve drills once a month and was not authorized for travel and lodging reimbursement.

While I was stationed at Camp Victory in Baghdad in July 2003, I was part of a team that eliminated Saddam Hussein's two sons, Uday and Qusay (who had a $15 million bounty). We did this in conjunction with Task Force 20 and with the aid of an informant that passed intelligence onto the 101st Airborne Division.

As the senior MP (Provost Marshall) in the entire country of Iraq, I was responsible for the brothers' remains and other evidence (such as their dental records captured by agents working for the Central Intelligence Agency (CIA)) that proved they were Saddam's sons.

Towards the end of that tour, on December 13, 2003, Task Force 121 captured Saddam. After initial integration, we kept him in a secret compound near Baghdad. That was quite a rewarding, exciting, and adventurous time for me.

After a short stay in Kuwait, we arrived at Camp Bucca, Iraq, near the Kuwaiti border in southern Iraq. At that time, I was in charge of Camp Bucca, the largest detainee operations facility in the world with over 20,000 detainees. Later, we moved up north to become the MP Task Force North. I worked near the same location where we held Saddam Hussein in a secret facility.

In 2005, I was honored to be selected to become the Commanding General for the 300th Military Police Brigade (BDE). After a few months of preparatory training at Fort Bliss, Texas, the 300th MP Brigade HQs (about 120 total officers, NCOs, and soldiers) were certified ready. Then we deployed to Kuwait for onward movement to Iraq in late 2007.

## My Personal and Business Life

I'm very fortunate and blessed to have a large, blended family. My wife and I have nine children between us. We have two beautiful daughters and seven sons.

Not only do I live by the Army Values, but I also passed these values along to my sons. Six of my seven sons joined the army right after high school. Two are still serving in uniform. My son, David, served one tour in Iraq and six tours in Afghanistan (as a Special Forces medic), earning six bronze stars, one with a "V" device for Valor. Another son, Adam, served multiple extended tours in Afghanistan. My sons, Tim and Phil, served during Operation Desert Storm (1990-91). Tim served again in Operation Iraqi Freedom in a precarious job as a turret gunner in an up-armored vehicle. His vehicle was hit by IEDs a few times, and he was eventually medically discharged from the army because of hearing loss. Zac (my stepson), my youngest son, didn't enter the military. His biological father left him enough money in his will to attend college. Zac's dad (Bill) was a highly decorated Marine Corps Pilot who flew Sikorsky Helicopters in support of Operation Desert Storm. Tragedy struck a few years later. After returning from Desert Storm, Bill had a massive heart attack and died.

Because we had a large family, I did not have the ability to help pay for my children's higher-level education. Because my sons followed me into the military, they were able to attend college thanks to the GI Education Bill. That was the same way I got my higher education!

Thanks to the GI Education bill, I have two Ph. D.s: a Ph.D. in International Business with a minor in human behavior and leadership and an honorary Ph.D. I also have three master's degrees and a couple of bachelor's degrees. I received those degrees while working a full-time job, attending night school classes, serving in the active Army Reserve, and raising a large family.

It took me five years of attending night school a couple nights a week and weekend classes to earn my Ph.D. I had achieved that goal by the time I was 35. When I was just starting and focusing on my doctoral dissertation, my employer (Lockheed) offered me a better job and more opportunities in the Bay Area, so we moved 500 miles north. Since my university was in San Diego, I traveled there to attend classes on Friday nights and weekends. I would jump on a Space-A flight on a Navy P-3 Orion originating out of NAS (Naval Air Station) Alameda and fly down to NAS North Island on the weekends to attend classes.

I found the leadership classes challenging, inspiring, and enlightening. I'm so glad I took those classes.

At the age of 35, I became an adjunct professor and taught night school classes for about ten years. I was inspired and excited to teach courses in accounting, finance, economics, business management, and leadership. I taught mainly at the National University and the University of San Francisco, the University of Phoenix, and Chapman University. I also taught business leadership and motivation classes to undergraduates and graduate students.

I worked at Lockheed Martin for 14 years and eventually became an Assistant Program Manager (APM) in the high-tech world. I tracked, monitored, and reported on government contracts. There's always an engineering lead or senior person running the program from the technical standpoint, and the APM does the important job of keeping the program and budget on schedule.

Then I moved to Cisco Systems for four years. I was an independent contractor working on-site in the finance department. I prioritized, rearranged, and scheduled my time to do my Active Army Reserve commitment and complete the Reserve Component Army War College (culminating in a master's degree in strategic studies). I studied at home from 9 p.m. to midnight every night in my upstairs office. I attended the active-duty portion at Carlyle Barracks in the summer months, which took two years to complete.

Because of these experiences, I have a well-traveled worldview as I have lived in and traveled through at least 50 countries. I have been to almost all the U.S. states, lived in

England and Canada, and visited Mexico and Central America. I can see how the two worlds of business and military integrate. Most CEOs only know the business side. They don't necessarily know the human dynamics side of the business. They don't necessarily know the optimal tactics, techniques, and procedures (TTPs) that lead a productive team. I've taught thousands of people under the most trying conditions: desert warfare, jungle warfare, arctic warfare, and waterborne operations. Compare that to leading a team of 50 people at a high-tech company where they might have ping pong tables, hoverboards, back massages, and free candy.

As you can imagine, I've lived a full life. Now, I want to give back to educate, empower, and inspire the next generation of leaders.

# Chapter 1
# Loyalty

*Bear true faith and allegiance to the U.S. Constitution, the Army, your unit, and other Soldiers. Bearing true faith and allegiance is believing in and devoting yourself to something or someone. A loyal Soldier supports the leadership and stands up for fellow Soldiers. By wearing the uniform of the U.S. Army, you are expressing your loyalty. And by doing your share, you show your loyalty to your unit.*

*ARMY VALUES*

As a military service member, you represent your country when you are in a foreign country, serving overseas, or serving at home. You're an ambassador for your country because you're wearing your country's uniform, and you're wearing our flag. People look to you as their representative of America.

Military members protect and provide assurance that we can continue living our great American way of life. All those people took a step forward, raised their right hands, and took a solemn oath to stand between us and any enemy that would attempt to take away our freedoms. My motto is "Not on my Watch." That means a lot to me. It was drilled into me the whole time I was in the Army. It is instilled over and over again into everybody in the military about being their country's representative.

## Loyalty to Your Team Members

My time in Vietnam was quite exciting. When you are 20 years old, you mistakenly think you are bulletproof and will live forever. Let me tell you about one of our many adventures that demonstrates our loyalty to one another.

We were loyal to each other because that's the way we were trained.

When conducting our information-gathering patrols, we were instructed not to engage the enemy unless our patrol leader (PL) gave us the okay to initiate contact. This prevents someone from getting trigger happy and compromising everybody on the team. When a potentially lethal situation arose, he would initiate fire with his CAR-15 and empty a 20-round magazine towards the immediate threat. We were instructed not to fire first because we were a small group of soldiers, and we had a limited amount of ammunition. We were operating deep in enemy-controlled territory and a Quick Reaction Force (QRF) to support us was not an option.

If the enemy started firing at us first, we could immediately respond and fire back.

Our job was to be quiet, stealthy, move slowly, and not be compromised.

The North Vietnamese Army (NVA) used a high-speed dirt trail on a ridgetop as a resupply trail on this one mission. We walked along ten to 15 yards downwards of the side of each trail and observed the trail looking up towards the top. On our second day in, we heard enemy activity on the trail.

We heard someone talking in Vietnamese. It sounded as if the voice was giving commands. We crouched, aimed our weapons towards the noise, and slowly and quietly moved our selector switches on our CAR-15 automatic rifles from safe to fully auto. We continued to watch and wait to see if we were compromised.

We heard and saw NVA soldiers walking down the trail. We had our weapons up at the ready. We were camouflaged. We were sweaty. The NVA soldiers had a flank guard on both sides of their patrol. The flank guard didn't see us. He came about 10 feet from us and paused. Then he started to relieve himself.

His AK-47 slung over his shoulder, pointing towards the ground. Suddenly, he caught our eyes, and we caught his eyes. He knew the second he saw us that our weapons pointed right at his chest. And he knew—and this was all instantaneous—that if he even tried to swing his weapon upwards, he'd be dead before he could raise it even halfway.

We waited for our team sergeant to engage first.

Our Team Leader (TL), SSG Mike Vanning, didn't engage, so we didn't engage. We trusted him because he was a draftee who took his service seriously. He became a Ranger and then went on to a combat leadership role. He was awarded a Silver Star.

The NVA soldier looked at all six of us with what I would call an I-can't-believe-what-I-seeing look on his face. He finally realized that he was at death's door. With his head down, he slowly zipped up his pants, backed himself up to the trail, and started yelling in Vietnamese. I don't speak Vietnamese, but I guess he said something like, "Holy Hanoi Jane, you are not going to believe that I just saw a group of enemy soldiers right there to our flank."

A column of NVA soldiers ran down the dirt trail past our position carrying resupplies and ammunition. We were still waiting for instructions from our TL to see how the situation developed. We didn't engage them.

In a blink of an eye, all of the NVA moved *di di mau* (quickly) down the dirt trail away from our team. Mike gave us the high sign to get the hell out of there PDQ (pretty damn quick).

All hell broke loose. About 30 NVA attacked us. We took off in the opposite direction, down the hillside. They pursued us. A running firefight erupted.

Fortunately, none of us were shot, injured, or hurt by hand grenades or anything else. We escaped and evaded the enemy. We put a lot of distance between them. After three or four hours we began to think they might have quit looking for us. We were relieved and excited that we finally got them off our trail.

We were in a triple canopy jungle, and there was no landing zone (LZ) big enough to land a Huey helicopter to extract us. This was 1970, way before the internet. We used our PRC 77 (AN/PRC translates to "Army/Navy, Portable, Radio, Communication") radios and talked directly to our Tactical Operations Center (TOC). The TOC had been monitoring our radio traffic ever since we were compromised. They alerted a quick reaction force (QFR) to be mobilized and flown out to help us. But you can't land a helicopter in a dense triple canopy jungle. We found a spot that was not so densely populated. We laid claymore mines flat on the ground in a big circle, then moved a safe distance away and used our handheld clickers to explode the claymores upwards into the triple canopy jungle. The explosion opened a hole big enough so the Huey helicopters could rescue us.

Three helicopters circled overhead. One at a time, the crew chiefs dropped down two 110-foot ropes on either side of their helicopter. The Huey helicopter did not have winches on them, so the ropes were just tied down and secured to the D-rings on the floor of the aircraft. As the first Huey helicopter came down lower to pick us up, the helicopter blades were chopping some of the tops of trees off, kind of like a giant flying weed whacker.

We all carried six feet of climbing rope and a carabiner (snap link) for emergency extractions like this. We used the rope to make a "Swiss Seat." We tied the rope around our waist and looped it through our groin. The carabiner was in front of us just about even with our belly button. Then we secured the 110-foot rope through the carabiner with a bowline. Our team leader inspected our knots to ensure they would not come undone. After his inspection, he looked up and gave the crew chief a big thumbs up.

The pilots lifted their collective control stick upwards as they hoisted us out of the jungle two at a time. After maneuvered up through the canopy, our heavy backpacks caused us to hang upside down. The three extraction helicopters, along with an escort of two AH-1 Cobra Gunships, took us to an emergency landing zone in the A Shau Valley, about an hour away. We were in groups of two, hanging upside down, spinning around in circles under the helicopter the whole time. I was excited and afraid. I wondered if the knots would come undone and we'd fall to our deaths. We each held onto each other's equipment to make sure nothing became loose.

We all survived that mission. That was August 6, 1970. To this day, we communicate with each other. We call that "upside-down day."

## Loyalty in Business

I was watching the *NCIS* TV show the other day. They brought in a new section leader for the group. His boss asked, "How are you getting along with your team?"

He said, "The team is doing okay."

Notice, he said, "the team." Not "my team."

In this *NCIS* story, bad things happen. They overcame it, and the bad guys were put away. At the end of the story, the new section leader said, "MY team is doing well."

That showed he bonded with the team.

I find that this situation frequently happens in the corporate world. You might take over as a leader of a team and people wonder, "What will their priorities be? Where is the emphasis going to be?"

Or you might have been promoted from within a group to lead the group. Your colleagues knew you as their friend. Now you are their boss. You have to adjust to this new role. In the Army, leaders who were promoted from the ranks were assigned to other sections specifically to overcome this familiarity issue.

They must know you have their backs.

## Having Your Direct Subordinates' Backs

When I was working for Lockheed Marine Systems in San Diego, I went to night school to get my Ph.D. I was on a tuition reimbursement program with the company. I would pay the tuition in advance. The company would reimburse me if I got a 'B' grade or better.

Money was tight. I had a large family with six kids. My wife wasn't working.

After one class, I got my B-plus, and I put in for tuition reimbursement. I was always on top of getting reimbursed. If the class ended on Friday and they reported grades on Monday, I put in the tuition reimbursement on Tuesday morning when I came to work.

I waited a week, and I hadn't received the check.

I waited another week, and I still hadn't received the check.

Not only was I out of that money, but I had to pre-pay for my next class.

I talked to my supervisor. He brought me to his boss, a man named Moe. He was the big boss not only in name but in stature.

He was a big, muscular man. He worked out with professional football players. He was intelligent and dynamic.

After Moe heard my story, he picked up the phone and called the HR person in charge of processing tuition reimbursements. He stood up for me. He used many foul words.

"If you don't send the check today, I'm going to rip your arm off out of your body. I'm going to smack you over your head until you're dead," he said to the guy on the other end of the phone line. Do you believe he said that?

I received my reimbursement check the next day.

Funny thing. From then on, every time I took a class and submitted the reimbursement form, I received my reimbursement check promptly.

Just like in the military, you can't jump the chain of command. I couldn't call the HR people and say, "Hey, didn't you get my reimbursement request? What's going on?"

I had to go through my supervisor, his boss, and the big boss.

I was very thankful that Moe spoke up for me and took the time out of his schedule to look after me because I didn't know what else I would have done. I might have had to stop going to night school, and I might not have ever received my Ph.D. Thanks, Moe.

I had so much respect for him. His actions inspired me. I knew that he cared for his people, and he was doing the right thing.

## Sticking Up For Your Team Members

"Bob. I'm completely blind. Not just legally blind but totally blind."

I couldn't believe these words from my engineering officer, Colonel Scotty. He was also so strong. He was a 7th-degree black belt in mixed martial arts. He could immobilize a person with two fingers. He had our unit record for doing 56 pullups on the chin-up bar. Scotty was a picture-perfect figure worthy of an Army Recruiting Poster.

But he had also gone on over 300 daily convoy missions on Main Supply Route (MSR) Irish which extended from Camp Victory to the "Green Zone" in Iraq, the most heavily assaulted and attacked route in Baghdad. Nearly every day as American convoys passed, he would see kids and civilians blown up by IEDs, their bodies lying on the streets and sidewalks.

To the insurgents, those kids and other civilians who were killed or injured were acceptable collateral damage.

He never got injured. His vehicle never got blown up, only shot at. While most up-armored vehicles can sometimes protect you from small arms fire, they can't protect you from emotional injuries. Those don't show up for a while.

About 13 years after we served together in Iraq, I called him for our annual Christmas call. I couldn't believe it when he said his eyes closed shut, and he couldn't open them. Physically, nothing was wrong with his eyes. But he suffered from what doctors call "conversion disorder."

Conversation disorder is a mental condition in which a person has blindness, paralysis, or other nervous system (neurologic) symptoms that cannot be explained by medical evaluation. Emotional trauma manifested itself by impairing his vision.

I talked to an associate and a friend of mine who does emotional healing therapy for veterans like Scotty.

She said a lot of times, veterans experience significant emotional trauma which they haven't processed or gotten out of their psyche, which is the human soul, mind, or spirit. They haven't dealt with it yet and processed the demons out of their minds.

Scotty went to Walter Reed Army Hospital six times and was seen by six doctors. They couldn't help him.

Then, they sent them to John Hopkins Hospital for six more visits with eye specialists. They couldn't figure it out.

He had emotional trauma so bad that it has impacted his life. His wife was his full-time care provider, 24/7. She took Scotty to doctor's appointments, special therapy sessions, and massage therapy. His tremors dislocated his jaw and caused his upper back to swell and dislocate.

They put in for aid and assistance, but the VA has denied him, saying he wasn't eligible. They even denied his appeal.

Here's a guy that's given a lot (26 years of his life dedicated to military service) for our country, and he's not been able to deal with the emotional trauma that he was exposed to during his time in the military.

Here's a person who served this country faithfully and loyally. Look at how he was being mistreated.

I think that's bunk. I went to my congressman and told him Scotty's story. He was working with Scotty's congressman to see if they could get that appeal turned around.

When you are part of a team, you stand up for your mates, no matter how long ago you were in the same unit.

When I last checked in with Scotty, he was receiving the proper treatment. He can now see so well that he is shooting targets and clay pigeons at his local rifle range.

## Questions to Educate, Empower, and Inspire

- Do you stick up for your team?
- Does your team know you stick up for them?
- How would they know how you stick up for them?
- Does your team have each other's backs?
- When did you see a team member show loyalty to the group?
- What can you do to build loyalty in your group?

# Chapter 2
# Duty

*Fulfill your obligations. Doing your duty means more than carrying out your assigned tasks. Duty means being able to accomplish tasks as part of a team. The work of the U.S. Army is a complex combination of missions, charges, and responsibilities — all in constant motion. Our job entails building one assignment onto another. You fulfill your obligations as a part of your unit every time you resist the temptation to take "shortcuts" that might undermine the integrity of the final product.*

***ARMY VALUES***

Twenty-eight UN workers were trapped on the rooftop of their three-story headquarters. They watched insurgents attack and set their compound on fire in Herat City in western Afghanistan. Our mission was to save them.

When I was in Afghanistan in 2004, during the first part of my year-long tour, I was assigned as the U.S. military representative to coach, teach, and mentor Abdul Rahim Wardak, the Minister of Defense for Afghanistan. He was a former Mujahideen commander who had fought the Russians. He's very highly decorated and was wounded seven times. He was a four-star general in the Afghan Army before the Russians invaded. He transitioned to the Mujahideen Army and fought the Russians as an indigenous fighter.

At that time, Afghanistan didn't have an army. They were putting all the pieces together and doing initial training.

In September 2004, President Karzai decided to replace a corrupt provisional governor in Herat City.

Herat City was the most prosperous and industrious city in Afghanistan. However, when trucks came in from Iran, the governor of Herat Province charged them a customs fee of $500-$1,000 to cross over into Afghanistan. He kept all that money and didn't pass anything on to the central government.

General Moeen (at that time, he was the senior Afghan Army General in charge of the fledgling Afghan Army) and I flew above Herat in a Blackhawk helicopter.

We saw the UN Compound under attack. Fire and black smoke billowed up as insurgents attacked the three-story building.

We buzzed the building a few times, landed on a flat roof nearby, and disembarked. We did an initial assessment.

I was the senior commander on the ground as a Colonel. The ground commander was Lieutenant Colonel Mike McMahon. He was a helicopter pilot and commanding officer of the 3/4th 3rd Brigade Combat Team, 25th Infantry Division, stationed in Hawaii.

He said, "Hey, why don't we go out in the street, try to quell this riot and insurgency, and talk to these guys? We should take our helmets off because if we come in full battle dress uniforms, they'll think we'll be ready for a fight, right?"

I agreed.

We took off our body armor and helmets. We didn't even wear hats or sunglasses.

We went out into the street and started talking to these guys with the help of our interpreters. Over time, a crowd of insurgents and other local nationals came.

This wasn't a good idea.

After a short time, the insurgents in the crowd started a gunfight and tossed hand grenades at us and into the assembled crowd. The crowd pummeled us with bricks and rocks. Mike got hit in the head with a brick and bled profusely. I got hit in the face with a brick which knocked me to the ground. I was bleeding and almost unconscious.

Mike and I retreated into the compound to protect ourselves. After things had settled down, we went to an aid station where they stitched up Mike's head and my face. Fortunately, our American troops, better known as Quick Reaction Forces (QRF), scattered the insurgents without killing anyone.

I directed the American troops (QRF) with up-armored vehicles to come in. We fought gallantly, and we got all the UN workers out of the compound safely. We were held in high esteem because we completed the mission without anybody being killed.

Mike and I received Purple Hearts and Bronze Stars with a "V" which means you were in close and decisive combat with the enemy. I was awarded my 2nd Combat Infantry Badge (CIB) from Major General Eric T. Olson, Commanding General of the 25th Infantry Division. Mike and I were also awarded the Amir Amanullah Khan Award from the Presi-

**Photo of BG Robert Hipwell, then a Colonel, after a dangerous Rescue Mission and firefight in Herat City, Afghanistan.**

dent of Afghanistan Hamid Karzai, the highest civilian award bestowed by the Government of Afghanistan.

As a footnote to the story, the insurgents decided that it wasn't worth the fight to keep the corrupt governor in place. So they faded into the woodwork, and we could transition to the new governor, who was loyal to the President. The new provisional governor ensured that commerce and business continued properly, and the Afghan government received its share of the tariffs.

But six weeks later, tragedy struck. A small plane piloted by a contract aircrew crashed into the side of a mountain during bad weather, killing all on board, including LTC Mike McMahon.

My tour of duty was up. Mike and I left the country the same day. However, Mike left the country in a pine box. I requested to escort his body on that aircraft, but they already had an escort assigned to take Mike's remains home.

## Questions to Educate, Empower, and Inspire

- Does your team go above and beyond? Or do they do just enough to get by?
- Do you do just enough to get by? Or do you go above and beyond?
- If you answered "yes," what inspires you to give it your all? If you answered "no," what would have to happen for you to want to contribute more?

# Chapter 3
# Respect

*Treat people as they should be treated. In the Soldier's Code, we pledge to "treat others with dignity and respect while expecting others to do the same." Respect is what allows us to appreciate the best in other people. Respect is trusting that all people have done their jobs and fulfilled their duty. And self-respect is a vital ingredient with the Army value of respect, which results from knowing you have put forth your best effort. The Army is one team, and each of us has something to contribute.*

*ARMY VALUES*

When I returned from Vietnam in 1971, I did not get a hero's welcome or anything close to it. American opinion about the war was split. Public opinion had turned against the Vietnam war effort and the military members who served there. Many people made derogatory comments about our military members and our veterans. Some people called returning soldiers "baby killers." Many TV shows and movies were derogatory toward the military. People didn't treat us with honor or respect. I didn't feel very good about the way we were treated, about how the media portrayed the warriors from Vietnam as heartless and cruel.

Like thousands of other veterans, I served my country faithfully and loyally and did my patriotic duty. But I had hidden my battle wounds where no one could see. Emotional trauma was bottled up deep inside me.

In Vietnam, the combat soldier typically served a 12-month tour of duty but was exposed to hostile fire almost every day. In World War II, the average age of a combat soldier was 26. In Vietnam, the average solder was 19. About half of the returning soldiers suffered from what psychiatrists call Post Traumatic Stress Disorder (PTSD). And even to this day, more than 50 years later, they continue to suffer.

According to a study conducted by the Veterans Administration, half of the returning Vietnam combat veterans have PTSD. Many vets complain of alienation, rage, and survivors' guilt. Some succumb to suicidal thoughts.

Almost 50 years later, many men are still fighting the Vietnam War. None of them received a hero's welcome. Honestly, I mainly suffered from survivors' guilt, alienation, and other emotional trauma as a young 20-year-old coming back from the "two-way rifle range." Every day, I saw death and destruction and the ugly side of war up close and personal during my tour of duty.

I don't remember getting any friendly greetings. Not even a "welcome back." No one thanked us. About 15 years later we received our welcome home when I attended a Vietnam Veteran appreciation celebration event sponsored by the 101st Airborne Division at Fort Campbell, Kentucky. We veterans led a victory lap ahead of the active-duty members and all our families. All my Vietnam Veteran brothers and I were applauded by the family and supporters seated in the stands as we walked by. At that small but emotionally thankful celebration, I finally began the emotional healing process, starting the path to recovery and a more normal life.

## Gratitude

My son, Philip, served in the Army with the 24th Infantry Division during Operation Desert Shield in 1990 and Operation Desert Storm in 1991. The U.S. had over 500,000 troops deployed to Saudi Arabia in case Iraqi troops attacked Saudi Arabia.

During Operation Desert Storm, the coalition pushed Saddam Hussein and his troops back towards Baghdad (about 500 miles north of the Kuwaiti border). They got halfway into Iraq, and they stopped. President Bush drew a line in the desert sand. He said, "We've got what we came here for, and we're going to leave."

They didn't kill Saddam. They left him in power but defeated him in battle. They achieved mission success by kicking Iraqi troops out of Kuwait and returning national sovereignty to the Kuwaiti people and government. At that time, Major General Barry McCaffrey, Commanding General of the 24th Mechanized Infantry Division (24th MID), announced, "Before we started our operation, Iraq had the second largest army in the world and when we finished our operation of liberating Kuwait, Iraq had the second largest Army in Iraq." The victorious U.S. Army was larger, more lethal, and more successful on the field of battle.

Philip and his fellow soldiers of the 24th MID and all our proud military were treated with love, respect, and gratitude. They were welcomed back a lot better than the returning Vietnam-era soldiers.

After about 11 months overseas, Philip and his fellow soldiers redeployed back to their home base at Fort Stewart, Georgia. As part of a representative group of the 24th MID, Philip was selected to go to Washington, D.C. for a victory parade in front of the White House.

He called me from Washington and said, "Dad, this is great. We marched past the President for review. People on the streets were thanking me and shaking my hand. We went into a bar afterward, and people bought us beers and pizza. Women were hugging and kissing us on the cheek."

I said, "That's good, Phil. I'm proud of you and very happy for you."

So soon after that, Phil and his unit were recognized by New York City with a Welcome Back Victorious Hero's ticker-tape parade.

They said, "Welcome back. You did a great job. You were very successful over there, and we're proud of you."

He called me from New York and said, "Dad, this is tremendous. People in New York are so friendly to us."

People bought them beers and pizza, shook their hands, and patted them on their backs.

We were living in San Jose, and Phil came to visit. A couple of days later, we went to Church together.

I was proud of Phil and asked him to wear his Class A uniform to Church that Sunday.

A couple of other young soldiers in the congregation had come back from Desert Storm and wore their Class A uniforms as well.

Before beginning his sermon, the pastor stood up and said, "I want to thank all these young men who fought in Desert Storm."

They got a standing ovation which was well deserved and justified.

When he sat down, I whispered, "Phil, this is great. I'm so glad you got recognized and appreciated for your sacrifice, hard work, and victory in Iraq. This didn't happen to us when we returned from Vietnam."

He turned to me and said, "I know, Dad. Thanks for the warm welcome back."

I couldn't have been prouder.

## Questions to Educate, Empower, and Inspire

- Do you thank your direct reports for their contributions?
- How did it make them feel?
- Have you done impactful work for your company but weren't recognized by your superiors? How did that make you feel?

# Chapter 4
# Selfless Service

*Put the welfare of the nation, the Army, and your subordinates before your own. Selfless service is larger than just one person. In serving your country, you are doing your duty loyally without thought of recognition or gain. The basic building block of selfless service is the commitment of each team member to go a little further, endure a bit longer, and look a little closer to see how they can add to the effort.*

*ARMY VALUES*

My son, David, served six tours in Afghanistan as a Special Forces (SF) medic. He and his team members had multiple, lethal engagements with the enemy.

For his actions, he was awarded six Bronze Stars and a Bronze Star with a "V" Device. The Bronze Star with "V" is awarded for valor or bravery during combat actions against an enemy force. It is the fourth-highest award for military combat bravery. After 26 years of faithful and loyal service, he retired in January 2021. He told me an amazing story of selfless service.

One of the soldiers he knew, Sergeant First Class Andrew Weathers, was shot in the head and critically wounded during a fierce firefight. They couldn't extract him right away because the gunfire was too intense. They ran out of ammunition three times, and they had to airlift ammunition to the team so they could continue fighting.

They eventually stabilized Andrew, and then they medevacked him to Landstuhl Regional Medical Center (LRMC) in Germany for more follow-up medical treatment.

Unfortunately, upon arrival, Andrew was considered brain dead. His parents flew to Germany to be with Andrew. An-

**Hero Sergeant First Class Andrew Weathers**

drew was not married. After an agonizing period, they decided to pull the plug and Andrew expired.

However, Andrew Weathers had signed the papers to be an organ donor.

I heard reports that Andrew helped 9 people who received his organs and body parts.

Even after his death, he continued to give to the cause of selfless service and help people by donating his body so others could continue to live better lives.

A service member doesn't want to think he gave his life for our country just to be forgotten.

So we always say, "Gone. But Never Forgotten."

## Do the Right Thing

My son, Mathew, an officer in the Army Nurse Corps, told me this story of a group that went above and beyond the call of duty.

He was deployed to Honduras when his unit was assigned to a medical mission to conduct several surgeries in Nicaragua in March of 2018.

Our countries did not have friendly relations then. So, there were all kinds of parameters to make this procedure possible.

There was restricted and limited airspace, and a limited time they could be in and out of the host country of Nicaragua.

Observers from the Nicaraguan Army got onboard each Blackhawk and Chinook helicopter alongside our troops to ensure they didn't go out of the airspace and did everything they were supposed to do.

They flew to a little village called Waspan on the northern border of Nicaragua and Honduras.

They had a three-day mission to help people that needed general surgeries for hernias, gallbladders, and other ileitis. They were on a tight schedule.

Near the end of the third day, a man came into the waiting room with his six-year-old son. The boy was crying and in pain. A poisonous snake had bitten him about a week earlier. His leg was gangly and black as the poison invaded his body.

Mathew was the team leader. He asked the team to work faster to have time to help this boy. He inspired his team because they only had a certain amount of time to work before the helicopters were scheduled to fly back.

The boy would have died from the snake bite. Fortunately, the surgical team removed the venom and fixed his leg. The U. S. provided a life-saving event for this little boy.

Mathew showed that leaders need to adapt to the situation and use their mental flexibility. Things happen, and life happens. You need to have the ability to adapt and overcome new obstacles.

## Questions to Educate, Empower, and Inspire

- What do you want to be remembered for?
- What will your legacy be?
- What will your team members remember you for after you or they move on?

**Photo of father (Robert) and son (David) leaving the safe house, going to visit the US Embassy in Kabul for a short and quiet respite.**

# Chapter 5
# Honor

*Live up to Army values. The nation's highest military award is The Medal of Honor. This award goes to Service-members who make honor a matter of daily living—Soldiers who develop the habit of being honorable and solidify that habit with every value and choice they make. Honor is a matter of carrying out, acting, and living the values of respect, duty, loyalty, selfless service, integrity, and personal courage in everything you do.*

*ARMY VALUES*

Honor has different shades, colors, and dimensions. Honor is multi-dimensional.

You can honor yourself by being forthright, taking the (sometimes difficult) high ground, and doing the right thing. You can honor your family by looking after and protecting your family, respecting your family, feeding your family, and sacrificing your time and energy to help and support your family.

Leaders in the Army tell you, "You're in the Army 24/7." That means you don't take the uniform off at the end of the duty day, and then later that night go to a public bar, get drunk, and do all kinds of crazy things. In fact, you are not authorized to go to a bar or other public establishment that serves alcohol and drink alcohol in a public setting while in your uniform.

From the military standpoint, your first honor is to the service you are in. It's a military system. It has the strict Uniform Code of Military Justice (UCMJ), rules, regulations, and doctrines that you must uphold every day of your life while you are in the military.

You must also honor your comrades in arms and the military and civilian personnel you work with daily. When you're in the field or cantonment (a military garrison or camp), you honor the soldiers next to you because they've got your back, and you've got their backs. You honor and respect them, and they do the same for you.

When you cross over into the corporate world, you must honor your company. First of all, they're paying your salary. You should do the honorable thing and be loyal to your employer. If you don't want to be there, move on and go somewhere else.

Some people may bad-mouth the company when they're sitting down at lunch with their co-workers or hanging around in your cubicle. Well, that's dishonoring the company. To work honorably at a company in corporate America, you need to be fully committed, loyal, and onboard.

Of course, like anything else, there may be a company policy or a corporate culture that you don't agree with. I don't think anyone is 100% comfortable or happy with a company or an organization all the time. But all that being said, they're paying your salary. They're providing your benefits for you and your family. You're increasing your experience and your skillset, so you should honor your company.

The bottom line: Honor is a key component, whether in the civilian community or the military community.

## Honor in Action

The highest military award is the Medal of Honor. Recipients have given selfless service and are a tribute and honor to the United States Army and the United States.

Sometimes a Medal of Honor is awarded for a single event or a battle that happened in a day or a couple of days. For example, in an intense fight where soldiers are in close quarters combat and decisively engaging the enemy, the recipient risked his or her own life, usually to save his fellow warriors from the jaws of death.

One such recipient is Sammy L. Davis, an Army Vietnam War veteran. His citation reads, "For conspicuous gallantry and intrepidity in action at the risk of his life above and beyond the call of duty. Sergeant Davis (then 21-year-old Private First Class) distinguished himself during the early morning hours while serving as a cannoneer with Battery C at a remote fire support base. Though suffering from painful wounds, he refused medical attention, joining another howitzer crew that fired at the large Viet Cong force until it broke contact and fled. Sergeant Davis' extraordinary heroism, at the risk of his life, is in keeping with the highest traditions of the military service and reflects great credit upon himself and the U.S. Army."

Sammy is one of several Medal of Honor recipients I know. He currently lives with his wife in Freedom, Indiana. On November 19, 1968, he received the Medal of Honor from President Lyndon Johnson during a ceremony at the White House.

Sammy's claim to fame comes from the movie, *Forrest Gump*. When you see footage of President Johnson awarding the Medal of Honor to Forrest Gump, you see part of Sammy's Medal of Honor award ceremony. In the film, actor Tom Hanks' (Forrest Gump) head is superimposed over that of Sammy L. Davis.

Here's another interesting tidbit: in the movie, Forrest Gump exposes his buttocks to the President. That did not happen in Sammy's ceremony. Sammy's nickname is "The Real Forrest Gump."

I recently saw a YouTube video where Sammy told the interviewer that you receive the Medal of Honor because you've risked your own life and did something above and beyond the call of duty.

The medal inspires him to live up to what it represents personally. "Because of the value I put on it, I've tried to be a better person," Sammy said.

Once you receive the Medal of Honor, you must always live up to the expectations of all the people who distinguish themselves with acts of bravery.

You have to be honorable for the rest of your life. People hold you in high esteem and they have high expectations of Medal of Honor recipients.

I would say you are in a fishbowl. You can't do things publicly that could demonstrate that you are unworthy of a Medal of Honor.

The military chain of command has the authority to issue awards to motivate servicemembers and increase morale. They have the same power to rescind awards if someone does something disloyal or dishonorable. The military chain of command will not tolerate anyone who diminishes the award with inappropriate behavior.

And neither should you!

## Questions to Educate, Empower, and Inspire

- Have you seen someone do an honorable deed, either in person or on TV? Describe it briefly.
- Have you seen someone do a dishonorable act in person? What did you do when you saw it? How did it make you feel?
- How would you create the feeling of honor inside your company?

# Chapter 6
# Integrity

*Do what's right, legally, morally, and ethically. Integrity is a quality you develop by adhering to moral principles. It requires that you do and says nothing that deceives others. As your integrity grows, so does the trust others place in you. The more choices you make based on integrity, the more this highly prized value will affect your relationships with family and friends and, finally, the fundamental acceptance of yourself.*

*ARMY VALUES*

Let me tell you about an inspiring man who is an excellent example of duty and integrity, General J.D. Thurman.

Think back to the early part of 2003. We were engaged in Operation Iraqi Freedom, which kicked off the second Gulf War.

I served in Kuwait in the command group of The United States Army Central Command, formerly known as the Third

United States Army Command. Our mission was to get ready for the upcoming battle in Iraq. We were waiting to get the green light from President Bush. We were stationed at Camp Doha in Kuwait. There was another new compound that the Kuwaiti Government was building for U.S. Troops. This new and improved compound in the grueling hot desert is called Camp Arifjan.

It was extremely hot—around 120 degrees during the day, cooling to about 99 degrees at night for most summer months.

Over time, Camp Doha got so busy and so crowded that you could hardly move around the camp. Coalition troops, U.S. soldiers, and Marines were everywhere. We didn't have enough barracks, so many people slept on cots or on the ground.

Going to the dining facility was a challenge because the lines were so long. You couldn't get in and get a seat with a buddy. You had to wait until a seat became available, then eat and get out quickly so someone else could sit down.

The main point here is we had 24-hour operations activity every day. I was the executive officer for General J.D. Thurman. He was a very hard-working general, and he spent an enormous number of hours working. He was the Corps Level G3 or Operations Officer responsible for the movement of all warfighting functions. This means he was the main staff officer responsible for all Corps Level Operations. A Corps consists of two to seven divisions and various support units with 50,000 to 300,000 troops and is commanded by a lieutenant general.

We were going over the operations plans, going to ranges, and testing firing our weapons as we were awaiting the green light from Washington to move forward.

Every day, we had two meetings. They were called BUBs, short for Battle Update Briefs, which General Thurman hosted.

I was the night-shift executive officer. I would come to the operations center at approximately six at night and work until about six in the morning.

Colonel Mark Clay was my counterpart. He would do the other half of the day. He or I would be with General Thurman and brief him and prepare him for his meetings. We would explain the highlights of the last 12 hours and explain current command priorities. We kept him posted on any critical updates or situations that needed his attention.

He had an extraordinary work ethic. Once we kicked off the offensive operations on March 20, 2003, he slept less than four hours a night.

He would leave the operation center after midnight every night. He always said in his Southern drawl, "I'm going to the ranch." Then he went to his quarters.

He would be back in that operation center by four every morning, fresh and ready to go—even though he had a heart condition. He wanted to make sure that things were happening the way they were supposed to happen.

His dedication to duty was unparalleled. I have never seen someone do that for such an extended period.

I was responsible for maintaining his classified email account. He had too much going on to read and answer emails. We told everybody to send BLUF emails, which stood for "Bottom Line Up Front." The General didn't need to know all the details. He had a saying, "Just tell me in 25 words or less why this is important."

I would review, prioritize, and filter about 300 emails every night. Kuwait is eight hours ahead of Pentagon time. People were still at work at the Pentagon in the middle of the night. They were sending classified emails to General J.D. Thurman, and they wanted a response ASAP so they could brief the senior leadership at the Pentagon. I would whittle them down to maybe ten or twelve emails and print them for him to read. When he came in at four in the morning, I would say, "Hey, General, these came in for you. These need your attention."

He would take a sip of his coffee and tell me how to reply to each one.

He told me, "Hey, Bob, if something urgent comes in from a senator or congressman or another high-ranking military official, I need to know that and what you told them." I was honored that he trusted me to respond on his behalf during this highly intense and critical time when many people's lives were on the line.

At that time, I didn't think much about the awesome responsibility General Thurman placed on me to let me answer his emails for him in his name.

I thought, "You have a job to do. You get it done."

Now, almost 20 years later, when I look back on this, I think that General Thurman must have had a lot of trust, confidence, and faith in me. Faith that I didn't see in myself at that time.

That's the sign of a good leader: They see the potential in their people that people don't yet see in themselves.

## Shouldering Responsibility

General Thurman kept to this grueling schedule. He dealt with the pressure of being on the cusp of the ongoing warfighting and managing the logistics for tens of thousands of troops. General Thurman was the hardest working general I've ever had the privilege of working with. I still admire him to this day. He was driven and dedicated to mission success, and his integrity was impeachable.

His integrity was 100%. He always focused on the mission and was faithful to his troops.

He wanted to ensure mission success and have minimal attrition in our troops. He did everything he could to ensure that our soldiers were fully supported and had all their mission requirements completed.

## The Day Operation Iraqi Freedom Began

We finally got the green light from Washington on March 19, 2003. We could move forward to take down Saddam Hussein. This was the beginning of what we would call, "Shock and Awe."

That night, the Air Force started their bombing missions and bombed a couple of presidential palaces and other strategic military targets in Iraq where they thought that Saddam might be.

They wanted to cut the head off the snake. But as we know now, that didn't work.

And then—this news still gets my heart pumping, even today—on the morning of March 19, 2003, General Thurman came into his BUB briefing. He said right away, "Okay, all you tankers, I want you to get your combat battle load of munitions loaded onto your tanks because we move out tomorrow morning at first light."

That was a very exciting time for me and all the other troops involved.

The following day we moved out. Camp Doha, Kuwait, was crowded. On March 20, the camp emptied quickly. All you could see was a billowing cloud of dust plumes rising in the desert sky as tanks and military vehicles rumbled north over the desert sands towards Baghdad. You could see tanks roaring ahead with helicopters supporting them.

It still resonates with me. It's a great event when you have 175,000 highly charged, highly motivated warriors streaming out of your camp in tanks and armored personnel carriers moving forward to engage with and defeat the enemy on their turf.

It was a Coalition effort. We had about 120,000 American Troops, Marines, and Army. There were 45,000 British troops. Also, Polish troops and Australian troops were going forward to Baghdad.

That's about a 500 mile-mission. We had to get the logistical support to provide fuel to help move those tanks and vehicles forward.

In about three days, we took complete control of Baghdad and its six million people.

That was a very exciting time for our country, civilian leadership, military leaders, and me. That was the big picture because I witnessed 175,000 troops moving forward, going into enemy territory, engaging, defeating the enemy in many big and small battles, and ultimately becoming tactically victorious.

**Photo of Saddam Hussein flanked by his 2 sons, Uday and Qusay. Taken at the height of Saddam's reign of terror.**

## Closing Comments

J.D. Thurman ended up becoming a four-star general. He had excellent leadership skills.

He had integrity and a sense of duty. General Thurman never used the "F-word." When someone messed up or didn't do something on time, he would never say anything derogatory about a person in a public setting. His favorite saying was,

"That dog ain't going to hunt," meaning that guy messed up and better do better next time.

Like many people from the south, he talked slowly. He would initially appear to be a slow talker and a slow thinker, and he would not overload you with many unnecessary words. But that was a facade. He was like the duck floating on the lake. The duck looks calm above water, but below the surface, he is paddling like hell.

After General Thurman's successful assignment as the Corps Level G3 or Operations Officer, he was selected as the commanding general of the 4th Infantry Division, the most high-tech division in the army.

He impressed me as a man who was always focused on the mission and dedicated to his troops.

He was one inspiring general. I look forward to following in his footsteps and being the kind of leader and person he exemplified.

As British Field Marshall, William Slim, explained, "The only test of Generalship is Success… The Soldier may comfort himself with the thought that, whatever the result, he has done his duty faithfully and steadfastly, but the Commander has failed in his duty if he has not won VICTORY—for that is his duty."

J.D. Thurman, as a man and as a general, had integrity and a sense of duty.

## Personal Integrity

Let's switch gears for a minute. When I think about people who have integrity, my wife, Cindy, tops the charts.

Before I redeployed to Iraq in 2007, the Army requested that every service member gives power of attorney to someone to manage his or her affairs. A limited power of attorney limits the power. And there's the general power of attorney that gives someone complete control. A general power of attorney gives an agent the power to handle your financial matters in your place. I gave my wife the general power of attorney because I had all the faith, trust, and confidence in her.

A month after I left on this deployment, Cindy decided she wanted to move from our house in San Jose (where we lived for 20 years) to a five-acre horse ranch in Granite Bay because she and our daughter were into horseback riding.

I had the most faith and confidence in my wife to do the right thing to buy this house and sell the other house. I didn't see that as a problem. But a lot of people might have had reservations.

We joke about that. My wife says, "If you don't retire soon, I'm not going to tell you where our new house is. When you come back you'll have to find us."

We laugh at that.

When I came back from deployment 11 months later, I found the right house, and my wife presented me with a shovel to muck out the stables.

I share this story with you because my wife is a perfect example of many Army values, including selfless service. She raised all those kids while I was teaching at night, away on deployment, traveling to many short-notice General Officer (GO) seminars, representing the Army at conferences and leadership training sessions, and presenting our nation's flag to a bereaved mother or father at a Final Military Honors Ceremonies.

I used to say, "My car spent more time in the long-term parking garage at the airport than it did on my driveway."

Every man should be so lucky to have a wife like my wife of 31 years.

## Questions to Educate, Empower, and Inspire

- Think back in your life (family, teachers, co-workers, leaders). Whom have you seen display integrity?
- What did they do that impressed you?
- How did their actions inspire or affect you?

Flying a leaders flyover mission over the city of Baghdad with CSM Akins 2008, observing many satellite dishes on the rooftops of buildings. During my first flight over Baghdad in early 2003, there we no satellite dishes on rooftops as they had been banned by Saddam and enforced by a death sentence if a citizen had a satellite dish.

# Chapter 7
# Personal Courage

*Face fear, danger, or adversity (physical or moral). Personal courage has long been associated with our Army. Physical courage is a matter of enduring physical duress and, at times, risking personal safety. Facing moral fear or adversity may be a long, slow process of continuing the right path, especially if taking those actions is not popular with others. You can build your courage by standing up daily and acting upon the things you know are honorable.*

*ARMY VALUES*

Personal courage to me means you do the right thing at the right time.

When there's a call for action, some people freeze. They run away, or they don't know what to do.

In the Army, personal courage means digging deep. You've been trained, rehearsed, and are ready to do what needs to be done to ensure mission success. And those actions might feel uncomfortable, or they might be ugly, or they might get you dirty. But you have to take those actions to ensure mission success.

In the army, they say, "Failure Is Not an Option." They repeat that message until it becomes embedded in your psyche. You cannot fail because people's lives are on the line. You're protecting your battle buddy next to you and defending your country.

Honestly, not everybody lives up to this ideal. But if you are a leader in an organization and you do not live up to it, then your team will not either. And they will have less respect for you. Your integrity and reputation are on the line.

So, personal courage means always doing the right thing in everyday situations and challenging situations. You must make sure you and your team accomplish the mission in the expected timeframe.

## Personal Courage in Action

During initial training as new generals (commonly called Charm School for Generals), they teach us there could be a pivotal point in your career when you decide to throw your stars on the table and say, "I don't believe this course of action is in the best interest of our country, and it goes against my own beliefs."

This is a story of when I had to throw my stars on the table.

When I was serving overseas on my last tour of active duty in 2007 and 2008, I was the Commanding General in charge of Camp Bucca in southern Iraq. At that time, Camp Bucca was the largest detention facility in the world. I had about 5,000 uniformed troops and about 5,000 contractors under my command. As a unified team, we were responsible for the care and custody of 20,000 detainees who were either a perceived threat or had attacked and killed Coalition Forces or civilians.

This period (2007-2008) was known as "The Surge" because General David Petraeus had ordered five additional Brigade Combat Teams (a BCT has a tactical force of about 4,000 soldiers) to "plus up" the force structure. Their primary mission

**Meet and greet with a local village leader at Camp Bucca, Iraq 2008. From left to right LTC Bush, Local Leader, BG Hipwell, Interpreter, CSM Akins.**

was to go into the city streets of Baghdad (based on actionable intelligence reports), kick in doors around 2:00 or 3:00 in the morning, and apprehend the suspected bad guys before they had the opportunity to cause death and destruction to Coalition Troops or civilians.

After these people were detained, they were transported about 500 miles south to the Camp Bucca Detention Facility for screening and processing. On average, detainees stayed 18 months before being released back into the population center where they were originally captured.

We worked and lived in a 40-acre compound next to Umm Qasr, a port city in southern Iraq. It stands on the canalized Khawr az-Zubayr, part of the Khawr Abd Allah estuary, which leads to the Persian Gulf. The port is separated from the border of Kuwait by a small inlet. A bridge across the waterway linked the port with Kuwait before the 1991 Persian Gulf War.

We had a massive facility. But we were supposed to be a passive Forward Operating Base (FOB) that only conducts routine defensive patrols around the perimeter for security purposes. Camp Bucca was a rear area detainee facility. Our focus and attention were primarily safeguarding detainees by conducting care and custody operations.

Our focus was to ensure detainees were safe, secure, and not causing any trouble. But we were getting attacked multiple times a week with mortars and 122 mm Katyusha rockets.

Case in point, when we were landing on the helicopter landing pad on December 25, 2007, we came under attack from 122 mm Katyusha Rockets. Luckily, no one was injured, but we were shaken up. The insurgents would launch surprise attacks into our compound with their unguided 122 mm Katusha rockets from neighborhoods in Umm Qasr. Many times, these attacks resulted in fatalities. Our troops, contractors, and detainees were killed and wounded.

The base didn't have a solid wall. Our outer perimeter was a berm and a tall wire fence inside the shelf, protected by concertina wire on the top. A green tarp hung over the fence. But over time, the hot winds and 120-degree weather tore into the tarp so you could see through the gaps, which we were always trying to repair.

We had observers in towers around our perimeter to observe insurgents at all times of the day and night. We had aerial drones the size of giant eagles equipped with cameras to see if they were coming in from outside. Unlike Rambo, we didn't use mines or explosives to ward off an enemy attack.

Our adversary's main target was the dining facility. Our mess hall was in the center of the compound. All uniformed personnel and contractors ate there. Our attackers wanted to inflict the maximum number of causalities. We had engineers reinforce the roof for extra protection. The dining hall had a reinforced double ceiling. In case a bomb struck and penetrated the first part of the ceiling, the bomb would not have enough explosive energy to penetrate the second protective layer.

But these 122 mm Katyusha rockets that attacked us were unguided. They usually went past the dining facility and hit the housing units used by the contractors, who were getting killed.

I kept talking to my boss, a two-star general, who was 500 miles north in Baghdad. I was on the phone with him all the time to keep him appraised of the current situation. He needed to know everything that was going on. He was communicating with me all the time. He told me, "Hey, stay where you are. Just hang low and stay down, and sooner or later, they'll stop shooting at you."

I thought, "I don't think so."

I didn't say that to him because he would say something inflammatory to me.

I thought back to my initial training for new generals. They warned us there would be a time when we needed to put our careers on the line. They told us we would need to decide to throw our stars on the table and say, "I don't believe this course of action is in the best interest of our country, and it goes against my own beliefs."

When you get a lawful order in the military, you've got to follow it. There's no doubt about that. I didn't get a direct order. He told me, "Bob, just relax. They'll slow down. They'll run out of rockets."

But that never happened. The insurgents never calmed down or stopped shooting at us.

I knew more rockets would come in, and more people would get killed. I couldn't let that continue unchallenged. Those were American people. American Troops. And those were my detainees. When you're in charge of detainees, you are responsible for their safety and wellbeing. For example, you can't even let them commit suicide. We had guys that tried to commit suicide. I could not have that happen. I had to protect my soldiers, my contractors, and my detainees.

I had an operations section and an intel section that did a lot of research and analysis. We sent patrols into the town of Umm Qasr to locate where the rockets were being fired. They recruited moles in the village. They talked to local people. They'd tell us, "The rockets coming from this house or this parking lot," or whatever. So generally, we knew where the rockets were coming from.

The insurgents had rocket launchers loaded on small pickup trucks. They would shoot a couple of rockets at our camp and then shoot again from somewhere else. They were elusive and very mobile. We had teams looking for them. They were under surveillance. We found out where they were launching most of their rockets from open spaces in nearby housing areas.

After gathering as much intel as possible, I ordered an attack against them before they could launch more rockets into our compound and kill more people. At midnight, we rolled out about 20 vehicles, surrounding and securing the area.

Our forward operations team took down a house that our intelligent reports indicated was where 122 Katusha rockets would be fired.

It turned out we had the wrong house.

The right house was next door. We didn't have a firefight per se or a battle like you see on TV. Our guys went in and secured the house. The bad guys took off with their rockets in their trucks, and they drove away about 40 to 50 miles north to Basra, and they never returned.

When my boss found out that I had ordered this counterinsurgency attack, he was furious with me. He got me on the secret red phone and lambasted me for over an hour. It was one of those calls when he did all the talking, and I just listened. He ranted and ranted for a very long time. Excuse my language. He said, "Bob, what the f*** were you thinking of? You're going to stir up the hornet's nest, and you will have more attacks than you ever had before."

He had been telling General Petraeus during his Battle Update Briefings (BUBs) that things were pretty calm down there at Camp Bucca. That bad things weren't happening.

But that wasn't the case. We were getting rocket attacks at least once a week. He was minimalizing any enemy activities at our location to our higher command. I was able to see the daily BUBs on my classified computer, but I was not on the agenda because my boss spoke for me and my current situation at Camp Bucca. Usually, at BUBs, you speak about exceptions and not about business as usual.

That's why I ordered that mission. I almost got relieved of duty that day. Honestly, he told me, "Bob, get the f*** in a helicopter and get up here right now. I want to talk to you face to face." However, the war was going on at high operations tempo. The helicopters had more urgent, high-priority missions than flying a general around. So I couldn't fly up to Baghdad, 500 miles away, for a couple more days. That was good because he had time to calm down.

I threw my star on the table. I exhibited personal courage. I did what I thought I needed to do as a general to complete my mission and keep my troops and detainees safe.

## Personal Courage in Business

I was offered a job at a small startup company as an independent contractor in Silicon Valley. The owner seemed like a decent, hardworking guy, and he had a good program going. I came aboard as the chief financial officer.

I quickly found out he was doing something unethical. At the end of the quarter, he wanted me to report inventory shipped that had not left the warehouse or even been moved.

At the end of each quarter, about 90% of the inventory "shipped" was labeled "shipped in place." But on the books, it looked like the inventory was shipped to customer sites even though it stayed in our warehouse. Then in the first quarter of the next month, it all came back as Return Merchandise Authorized (RMA).

I said, "Hey, this is not right. You can't do this. It is not within accounting standards. It's not ethical."

He said, "I've been doing this all this time, Bob. What's the matter with that?"

I said, "You can't do it."

He said, "I'm going to do it."

I said, "You know what? You'll have to find somebody else to keep your books because I'm not going to work here." I left. I couldn't do that.

I could have said, "Okay, I'll doctor the books like you want so I can keep my job. I'll keep my head down and just continue to get my paycheck." But I couldn't do it. I moved on and went to another company. That's an example of personal courage and integrity in business.

## Questions to Educate, Empower, and Inspire

- Have you ever seen anyone in your business career display personal courage? What did they do?
- Have you ever seen anyone back down in the face of personal courage in your business career?
- What did that action do to you or your team?
- How would you instill a sense of personal courage in your team?
- What resources would you need to make this happen?

# Chapter 8
# Leadership

Let me tell you about an inspiring leader, Lieutenant General William Webster. In early 2003, I was an operations staff officer working with the staff of the Third Army, Camp Doha Kuwait. William Webster (then a Major General) was the Deputy Commanding General of the Third Army and all ground forces for Operation Iraqi Freedom.

He was a dynamic and aggressive leader. He was forthright and upcoming. For example, before we kicked off, there was an anthrax threat in Iraq. We were required to get anthrax shots. Some soldiers and military people were reluctant to do that.

We heard rumblings from the troops saying, "I don't know about anthrax shots. Maybe the shot will have side effects. Maybe we'll have six-toed babies down the road."

In the military, we say leaders lead by example. So, one day General Webster made a point of getting his anthrax shot. He volunteered to go to the head of the line. He rolled up his sleeve and got the anthrax shot. He showed all the troops a two-star general getting the anthrax vaccine.

He told them, "Don't worry about it. It's not going to kill you. You need it because we're going into an environment where anthrax might be used, and anthrax might kill you."

He led by example.

## Logistics

To me, it seemed like General Webster was always in the Ops Center, working with the teams that were getting prepared for the upcoming fight, and making sure that all the rehearsals, range firing, and logistical support activities were lined up and ready to go on time. Supplies and fuel would be there when the soldiers and troops needed them.

As the tanks, artillery, and armored personnel carriers rolled out fully combat-loaded, he was always on top of the situation, ensuring that they were fully supported.

## Innovation

In the summer, it was 120 degrees in the hot desert of Southern Kuwait. Since we had so many helicopters and not enough adequate landing pads, all the helicopter landing pads were sand. When you land a helicopter in the hot desert sand, you will get a lot of flying debris that could choke out helicopter engines.

Webster thought of a terrific solution. He used Rhino Snot (a soil stabilizer used everywhere from golf courses to airfields) on the helicopter landing zones. Rhino Snot will penetrate the sand and soil to bond the sand and soil particles into a solid mass. It worked! He protected our troops, pilots, and crews.

General Webster thought of another great idea. In 2003, the Army had just come out with a Blue Force Tracker (BFT), a transponder you put in your vehicles so that friendly forces could track friendly forces.

But we barely had enough blue force trackers to go around.

General Webster came up with a clever idea. He said, "That's an easy fix. Let's put a blue force tracker on the lead vehicle and another on the tail vehicle. That way, we would know that the vehicles between those two vehicles are friendly troops, so we don't attack our friendly troops."

To keep his troops safer, he was adamant about getting as many BFTs as soon as possible to protect and save us from friendly fire.

## Communication

General Webster was a very inspirational general. He helped create an integrated workspace environment to monitor and get up-to-date status on all our main counterparts: aviation, engineering, military police, combat units, and artillery.

Desks and workstations, each with multiple computers and monitors, were arranged in elevated rows in an amphitheater -style setting. We had a large, movie-type screen upfront, made up of separate smaller screens aligned next to each other. There were about five screens (each screen was about 4x4 foot square) aligned horizontally and five screens (4x4 feet square) aligned vertically. So, we had about 25 screens aligned next to each other. Each screen was assigned to individual staff sections, which displayed up-to-date information such as the amount of fuel available and the number of ships in port discharging resupplies.

He allowed one major news network to see this setup, which is a rarity in the military because you want to keep operational security and not broadcast your intentions to the enemy. They were able to video and take pictures. They agreed not to broadcast the video live and had to wait until it was decided that broadcasting the setup would not impact operational security and put friendly troops in harm's way.

When we did have the Shock and Awe, they merged all the screens except one, CNN, so we could see aircraft flying over Baghdad. We couldn't see the aircraft per se. We could see little white dots moving across the screens in different directions as aircraft took out critical strategic military targets in Baghdad. We knew exactly where all the aircraft were.

From my perspective, it must have been an air traffic controller's nightmare with so many aircraft in the air, going in different vectors, and conducting bombing missions. Visually, watching the mission was as though you hit a hornet's nest with a stick, and the hornets were buzzing around everywhere. Our air traffic controllers did a good job that day directing air traffic, and all our aircraft returned safely.

That was very exciting, and we were very successful. We didn't have as many fatalities or casualties compared to the Vietnam War or other major combat actions.

In fact, some Iraqi generals in Southern Iraq knew that the Iraqis would get annihilated when the war began because our superior military forces began their march north to Baghdad. The local Iraqi leaders made secret deals with our senior military leaders to capitulate and surrender as soon as the lead elements of our forces rolled through their areas of responsibility. The leaders surrendered as agreed with minimal causalities.

A couple of those Iraqi generals were considered high-value detainees (HVDs). We detained them in a special detention facility for about a year. Eventually, they were released and went back to their families.

I respected General Webster very much for his ingenuity and his ability to lead troops in combat.

## Questions to Educate, Empower, and Inspire

- Do you show up first for your team and lead by example?
- How does your team react when you do?
- If you haven't led by example, why haven't you?

# Chapter 9
# Morale and Corporate Culture

"It's another great day in the AOR (Area of Responsibly) and another great day for the 101st."

That's how General David Petraeus started our day in the AOR, which included more than 12,000 troops spread out over an area the size of a small state. He constantly inspired his troops with his positive attitude. He always came on the radio and said at the opening of his daily Battle Update Briefs (BUBs), "It's another great day in the AOR and another great day for the 101st."

You've all heard of General Petraeus, who led the American forces in Iraq. I served with him for quite a while. I served my second tour in Iraq with him in Baghdad in 2007 and 2008 during "The Surge." He was the four-star general in charge of everything in Iraq and the surrounding regions. I attended his Battle Update Briefs (BUBs) near Baghdad in the Al Faw Palace. The three-story Al Faw Palace was converted into a four-star command HQ (also known as the Water Palace) and was located in Baghdad, approximately three miles from the Baghdad International Airport on the U.S. Forward Operating Base (FOB) known as Camp Victory.

Of course, in combat, bad things happen. He always had a positive attitude despite the ugly side of combat. During that time, with the high operational tempo and constant combat action, we all knew that some people would be killed, a helicopter might crash, and insurgents might attack a military compound or blow up some vehicles with Improvised Explosive Devises (IEDs).

But General Petraeus would always start with a positive statement (which became his signature statement) and say, "It's another great day in the AOR. Another great day for the 101st."

He was saying that he was looking for good things from his troops. He's the Commanding General of the world-renowned 101st Airborne Division, so he set the example and the atmosphere.

His signature saying still resonates with me almost 20 years later. "It's another great day in the AOR and another great day for the 101st."

Another thing I admired about General Petraeus is that he was always in top physical shape.

One day earlier in his career, General Petraeus went to inspect his troops at a training range where his soldiers were shooting live ammunition on a "shoot-and-move" rifle range. One of the soldiers tripped, fell, and mistakenly had his finger on his trigger. When the soldier went down into the prone position, he prematurely pulled his trigger and shot General Petraeus in the right side of his chest, right above his name tag.

General Petraeus was air evacuated to a nearby hospital outside Fort Campbell in Kentucky.

Two or three days later, he told the doctor he wanted to be discharged.

The doctor wanted him to stay and continue to recover from his gunshot wounds.

The General said he had recovered enough and wanted to return to his troops and complete his mission. So, to prove to the doctor he was physically okay, he got down on the floor and did 50 consecutive push-ups.

The doctor soon released him.

So, here's an Army Officer and leader who had been shot a few days earlier right in his chest with a military-grade 556mm 5.56 AR-15 Rifle. He got down and did 50 push-ups consecutively, then returned to work because he wanted to be back with his troops, be the leader, and lead by example.

That's an inspirational leader. When people find out that someone has done something like that, they want to get right back to work and not make excuses about why they can't come to work.

Troops and subordinates say, "If our leader can do that, then I can get up off my ass and do something that is expected of me and complete my assigned duties today before I go home." He wasn't someone who would milk it and stay in the hospital for as long as possible.

He's a very inspirational leader.

Let me share two more stories about General Petraeus that show how he built morale and culture.

During his tour of duty in Iraq, a Personal Security Detail (PSD) consisting of 32 highly trained and highly motivated Military Police members from my command, guarded and protected him 24/7. He would do a three- to-five-mile run around the military base almost every afternoon when he had some downtime in his schedule.

He had an armed guard in an armored vehicle ahead of him and an armed guard in an armored vehicle behind him. He would selectively invite troops to run with him almost every time.

To inspire the troops, he held contests to see who could do more push-ups. Younger soldiers would say, "Hey, I can do more push-ups than General Petraeus."

And some people can. But the challenger always had to do them in cadence with Petraeus. The General would do ten fast push-ups, pause for a couple of seconds, do ten more push-ups, and pause for a couple of seconds.

Most people couldn't keep up with his stamina. He had athletic durability. With his running and with his pushups, he led by example.

In the military, you must be physically fit to do your job and stay healthy. The troops knew he was physically fit. They could see him running around the compound when he had downtime, even though he worked very long hours.

My MP troops would tell me sometimes that he would be on his way to bed after a day full of meetings… but all of a sudden, he would get a call from the Iraqi ambassador or another high-ranking Iraqi official because something bad had happened or something might be wrong unless immediate action was taken. He would put his uniform back on and travel with his PSD Team and meet the Iraqi ambassador for two hours or more and get back late at night. He would get up early again the next day for work and lead by example.

He was a very dynamic guy, very hard-charging, and a very charismatic leader.

He would never lambast anybody in public. If something wasn't going the right way, he would sternly but politely tell them to check their facts and get back to him ASAP. If you're talking to a four-star, you better have your facts 100 percent lined up because the senior leadership has to make strategic decisions that might affect troops in life and death situations based on your information.

## Company Culture

I consulted for one of the biggest Silicon Valley companies which had many modern four-story buildings. They always tried to give their individual contributor employees window cubicles. The managers had interior offices without windows.

That's one way to promote esprit de corps and improve employee morale.

However, corporate culture might differ at other companies to fit their vision statements.

Typically you go into somebody's office, and there's a picture of a loved one, a family member, baseball memorabilia, or something of interest to the person.

At that same company I consulted with, none of the managers or directors had any family photos in their offices.

The corporate culture was such that they didn't want you to focus on something outside of work.

Many companies in Silicon Valley have many amenities onsite, so employees never have to leave campus. They have free food. They have yoga classes at lunch. They have hair salons.

They even have a car wash and car repair shops available to all employees on campus.

They had all kinds of services to provide to the employees because they didn't want them to leave the campus.

What does the way you treat your employees say about your company culture?

## Questions to Educate, Empower, and Inspire

- Do you project that same respect to your direct reports?
- Do they see you as a person to emulate?
- If not, what can you do to become the type of leader that people admire and want to follow?

# Chapter 10
# Dealing with PTSD

You've probably heard of PTSD. But you probably don't know what it means or how it affects soldiers.

The National Institute of Mental Health defines Post-traumatic Stress Disorder (PTSD) as a disorder that develops in some people who have experienced a shocking, scary, or dangerous event.

Here is my PTSD story.

Survivor guilt was my overarching problem.

For me and most of us in Vietnam, we never had closure. When someone got wounded and was evacuated to the Army Hospital in Japan, we never heard anything about him other than he was gone. We never got closure about our comrades in arms especially those comrades killed in action (KIA).

We would ask questions, and nobody seemed to know any answers. So for me, having been in combat, I was under a lot of stress. I had seen a lot of carnage. We had horrendous attrition in my unit. We had many people killed and wounded. While I was on R&R, my teammate, Kenny, sustained three gunshot wounds from an AK-47 in his stomach and was air evacuated out of Vietnam. I never heard an update on his condition. About ten years later, I found out that Kenny died from complications from his injuries. Ken was 20 when he was shot.

I had just gotten married during a recent seven-day R&R in Hawaii. My new wife was pregnant (but I didn't find out until later) with our honeymoon baby but didn't tell my parents. I didn't know for sure if I was ever coming back because I was going back into the belly of the beast, where many of my buddies were taken by the beast.

So, I had a lot of stress. I wasn't sleeping well. I was in a high operations tempo mode and going on back-to-back missions in and out of the field. I had early signs of PTSD, but they didn't call it that back then. The powers-that-be called it "battle fatigue." I was very upset. I was irritable. So they had me do a psych evaluation.

They sent me back from Vietnam to a military hospital in Fort Ord, California, in late January 1971.

I was in the hospital for a while. The doctors did a psych evaluation on me, and they gave me some drugs to calm me down. As I mentioned, combat soldiers never get deep REM sleep while we were in the bush. You only get to a small level of sleep because you're always alert and semi-awake, especially when you're constantly surrounded by the five other guys in your unit 24 hours a day. At least one of you is always awake, and you pass the guard shift at night from one guy to the next.

And if something sounds out of place or you hear noises in the bush nearby, everyone wakes up.

I was stressed out.

They released me about two or three months later. Because my three-year contract was just about up and the army was downsizing significantly, they let me out a couple of months early. I got an honorable discharge and everything else that comes with doing a dedicated, faithful service.

Soon after that, I got a phone call from a guy at the CIA.

He knew I was an intelligence collector and worked with the CIA and other government intelligence agencies.

He asked me if I wanted to work for the CIA.

And having had a newborn baby and a two-year-old son. I said, "No thanks."

I don't want to return to that environment and potentially leave my new family for long periods of time.

We never got closure back then. Today, if a battle buddy gets killed in combat, typically the unit will have closure in the battle area and have a final remembrance ceremony. The local unit members get the chance to honor and respect the life of one of their own. They know that if they die on the field of battle, they too will be honored for their ultimate sacrifice.

I hope this has given you a small indication of what PTSD is, how it affects people, and why you, as a leader, can be more sensitive to your veteran workers who might be living with PTSD.

## Questions to Educate, Empower, and Inspire

- Does your company offer counseling services for veterans?
- Do you make accommodations for veterans who have issues—hidden or visible?
- Does your company appreciate veterans?

# Chapter 11
# Teamwork

Would you ask an up-and-coming Army general to pick up lunch for the team?

That's precisely what the founder of a startup I worked for asked of me.

And I gladly picked up lunch because it was the right thing to do to support the team and get the job done.

Here's why.

We infantry types, better known as "grunts," say there are only two types of people in the army. There's the infantry and those that support the infantry. But, on the other side of that coin, the supply guys say, "Bullets don't fly without supply. You'll need us as soon as you run out of ammo and chow."

In 1998, I was still committed to my active Army Reserve career, and I attended weekend meetings once a month and two-week summer camps once a year. My Army Reserve

Special Forces unit had many other short-term additional missions assigned to them from higher HQs. These missions were often overseas to the Republic of Korea and other undisclosed locations.

Concurrent to this period, I was working full-time for a high-tech startup company with six employees in Palo Alto. I was the only person that was not an engineer. Four of these guys were young, recent Stanford engineering graduates. The boss was 20 years younger than me. He had a vision and a plan to develop superior, low-cost fiber optic components. I respected him and admired his vision.

I was primarily a finance guy. My job was to cover all the bases other than the design engineering, including HR, scheduling Tech Shows, keeping the books, and paying their salaries and the rent.

We moved from our incubator site in Palo Alto to a small facility. Soon after we arrived, the founder said to me, "Hey Bob, I want you to go out every day at lunchtime and get sandwiches for these guys because I don't want them screwing off and spending an hour-and-a-half trying to get lunch." He wanted them to stay focused on the engineering design effort and work together, get more bonded, and focus on our fledgling startup company to develop a superior fiber optic product to make a profit.

I got these guys lunch every day because of what the boss said to me. I fully respected him. I fully respected the focused technical ability of these young start-up engineers. They needed to get the design finalized quickly to move to the manufacturing phase and get our product out the door before running out of venture capital. I was putting my ego aside because doing so builds character, teamwork, and a feeling of accomplishment.

Simon Sinek wrote a book called *Leaders Eat Last*. I believe that's the case. Leaders should leave their egos at the door and do what will help the team succeed.

Leadership and teamwork are all about getting the job done. I learned this hard way in Vietnam.

**The author (BG Robert Hipwell), with some of his key staff members, briefing General David Petraeus during his visit to the 300th Military Brigade Headquarters located on Camp Victory, Iraq in August 2008.**

## Teamwork In Action

In Vietnam, I was on a long-range reconnaissance patrols (LRRP) team. These are mostly used for recognizance and surveillance-type operations. This was long before we had satellites, drones, and other high-tech surveillance equipment. We were what intelligence circles called "their eyes and ears with our boots on the ground up close and personal." Sometimes we would confirm or deny what aerial photos were telling intelligence analysts.

We were configured into six-man teams. Huey helicopters, escorted by a hunter-killer team consisting of two Cobra Gun Ships and a low-flying two-man Loch helicopter, would air assault us deep into enemy territory. We'd stay for five to seven days.

Our main mission was to radio back any activity that we saw. We're constantly communicating with our Intel and Operations Center. We are looking for what we call "actionable intelligence." If we found something big that Higher Headquarters wants to destroy or disrupt, they would extract us. Then they would call for an airstrike. Airstrikes were usually 500-pound bombs dropped by B-52 Bombers. This was called an "Arch Light Strike." Then about 24 hours after the Arch Light Strike, they would insert us in a new location. We would conduct Battle Damage Assessments (BDA) and radio back what we saw or didn't see, like the absence of resupply vehicles and fresh troops moving southward along the Ho Chi Minh Trail.

Our job was not to make any contact with the enemy whatsoever. It was just to be quiet, go slow, observe, and report back. Once we got back, the division intelligence section would debrief us on the whole mission.

An LRRP Company is a high-operation tempo unit. Things moved quickly and sometimes unpredictably. Everybody volunteered to be in this type of unit. Before I went to Vietnam, I had gone to advanced training, including Ranger School and Recon Commando School.

Once I got there, I was assigned to a team as the assistant patrol leader (APL) and as a Sergeant (E5). Our Patrol Leader (PL) was a Staff Sergeant. I studied and learned from him, and he mentored me as he had much more experience and time in the jungle. Four other heavily armed soldiers were on the team.

We worked together. We trained a lot while we were not in the jungle. We typically had five to seven days out and two to three days back. The first day we returned, we were all happy to take a shower.

Our Standard Operating Procedure (SOP) was initiated as soon as we received our new mission brief. We all stopped taking showers and shaving, especially not using aftershave lotion and other personal hygiene products, so we wouldn't smell like a perfume factory in the jungle. When we returned from our missions, we needed to decompress and get a good night's sleep because we never got any deep, REM sleep in the field. As the old saying goes, "You have to sleep with one eye open."

In the jungle, we move very slowly, trying not to make any noise or get snagged in the underbrush.

We all carried an approximately 100-pound rucksack (oversized backpack). We carried our usual array of weapons such as CAR-15s (automatic rifles), M60 machine guns, a 7.62 mm sniper rifle, M79 Grenade launcher, PRC-77 radios with extra batteries, additional ammunition (four each M67 frag grenades, two claymore mines each), and other supplies. Each man carried about 100 rounds of extra 7.62 mm MG (machine gun) Ammo.

The Patrol Leader and the Assistant Patrol Leader were issued a couple of highly controlled morphine syringes which were only to be administered in case of a severe injury, such as a gunshot wound. We also carried five days of LRRP rations—one meal a day. Most times, we would bring cans of C -ration peaches rolled up in a long green boot sock (so the cans would not make noise) and a five-day supply of water. On a mission, you are on constant alert for danger. So, we needed a day to decompress, rewind, recover, and drink a beer or two.

But the other two days, we trained. We always worked together, always knowing each other's strong points and weak points so we could anticipate any problems we might have in the field. For example, I am a left-handed rifle shooter. So, most of the time, I would guard the right side of the trail because my weapon would be ready to bring it up. A right-handed shooter would have his weapon slung for the left-hand side so he could look on the left-hand side of the trail.

We all lived in the same Quonset huts. We went to chow together. We exercised together. We watched movies on a reel-to-reel outdoor movie projector together. We trained together as a team. We became an effective and cohesive team.

We practiced. We rehearsed. If we got ambushed from the right side, what would happen? If we got ambushed from the left side, what would happen? Of course, whatever happened out there was going to be unique. But we have scenarios for as many scenarios as we could come up with.

Standard Operating Procedures (SOPs) need to be ingrained in your muscle memory so that if something happens in the field, you do not have to think about it. "Is this a life-or-death situation?" You must make decisions based on what is coming at you to negate that situation and be victorious, come through, complete your mission, and get everyone out of there safely.

It happens automatically. Instinctively.

In a combat situation, you are trained to expect specific scenarios. You train and train and train some more—and rehearse and train. So, when something *does* happen, you automatically go into reflex mode. You react based on your reflexes or muscle memory. Later, when things calm down to a certain extent, you start to think about it logically.

Most combat is engaged by young people—under twenty-five. In one respect, you almost feel bulletproof at that age. The fear of dying is not there like it is when you get a little older and think, "Oh man, what was I thinking? Why did I do that?"

So you've got that young, eager "that won't happen to me" thought in your head. But other people on other teams are getting killed and wounded, and you know that could happen to you.

However, because of your training, your expertise, and your confidence in the men around you, you think that they are going to look after your back and you're going to look after their backs. You think you're going to be okay.

Training teaches you to get out of your way. That thinking part can set up that extra bit of time that can make the difference between life and death. That extra split-second is removed because you know instinctively what to do.

Six of us are out there. But we are acting as one unit, one team. Our constant training took us to another level.

Even before we go out in the field, there is a two-to-three-day preparation period. For example, in the jungle, everything smells dirty and rotten. So once our mission was assigned to us, we stopped taking showers, brushing our teeth with toothpaste, or putting on any froufrou smells. After three days, you smell so bad.

We are already stinky by the time we go out to the field. We do this because your senses get alerted when you're out in the field. They go to a higher level. You can smell things in the jungle that you wouldn't smell otherwise. We did not want the enemy to smell any pleasant scents from deodorant, toothpaste, or shampoo.

We thoroughly prepared our equipment to make sure it did not rattle or make metallic sounds. For example, we taped a cigarette butt to the dust cover of our weapon in case we had to pull the charging handle to cock it or move it so it would not make a metallic sound when the dust cover opened.

You always go out to the field sterile. Everything on a uniform is taken off. No U.S. Army insignia, unit patches, ID Cards, and no wallet. In Vietnam, we received Military Payment Certificates (MPC) money (kind of like Monopoly money) because the U.S. government didn't want millions of U.S. dollars to get into the wrong hands. We did not even wear our dog tags around our necks. We laced them in our boots. And the last thing we ever wanted to do was take a letter from a girlfriend or a spouse. Sometimes in the rear, when you get lonely, you want to pull out that letter and reread it and reread it. But in the field, we would never do that because that would compromise us if we ever got captured.

We shook and inspected each other. We had to rely on each other.

Our job was to be quiet, stealthy, move slowly, and not be compromised.

We typically moved very slowly. We would move for about 50 minutes and stop for 10 minutes to rest and catch our breath so we would not get impatient and fight to get unsnagged from the undergrowth. We usually had three to five teams out in the area. Each team was assigned a predetermined area of responsibility, usually within a three-to-five-mile box on the map. We used handheld, lensatic compasses to navigate. This was way before GPS was invented.

When we're out in the jungle, we don't talk at a normal conversational level—unlike Hollywood movies. There's no such thing as talking when we're on patrol in enemy-controlled territory because sound carries a long distance, even in a triple-canopy jungle.

You whisper very softly. We would use hand and arm signals. Anything we would say in a normal voice would pass through the jungle. It would not be a legible conversation, but our words would be identifiable as talking. There's always a certain amount of noise that will come through, and you never really knew how far the enemy was from your location.

If you've been in an area for a while, you know the normal sounds. If you hear someone talking, even if it's in a different language or a couple of words, that will alert you that someone is nearby.

We took all our water with us. We carried two-quart bladders of water in our rucksacks. We didn't want to go down to the creeks because that's where the enemy would go. If somebody opened a canteen, we'd pass it around the group so water wouldn't make noise while we moved on our trails. Yes, we all drank from the same canteen.

The last guy on the trail would cover up our tracks. We would try not to break branches and twigs to make sure that we wouldn't be followed. We would trade off carrying the heaviest machine guns.

We'd move a mile a day from one location to the other—slowly. We would never stay in the same spot twice. We would never sleep in the same area twice.

When it got dark, we stopped at one place for a while. Then we would leave that place and go to another place for the night. Using military terminology is (RON) rest overnight. So, if the enemy was watching us in the jungle, and they go, "Oh, they're over there by those trees," we wouldn't be there because, after dark, we moved to our RON position. We would look for a small, concealed area with heavy vegetation and set up for the night. We camped in a triple-canopy jungle, the thickest, darkest place we could find.

We never made a small campfire because it would alert the enemy to our position. Often, we were able to observe and report enemy activity based on their campfires. The smells of their food would come downwind to us. We ate long-range rations: you put water in a condensed food packet and ate it. We ate cold food. Only one or two of us would eat simultaneously because the other four men would have to make sure that we could guard the perimeter if we were attacked.

We had to know where all of our equipment was at all times. It takes a while for your eyes to adjust to the darkness. Even after half an hour of being in a triple-canopy jungle at night, you don't get much visibility. Back in the Vietnam era, we did not have night vision devices (NVDs).

We were never going to turn on a flashlight at night so that we could see things.

So when we sat down and set up for the night, we had to know where our hand grenades were so we could have them within reach if we needed to reach for them in the middle of the night. We would know exactly where they were.

We slept with our feet facing towards the middle of a circle, like a wagon wheel, and we each faced outward to see if we could detect any enemy nighttime activity. Many times, the NVA would use white flashlights at night, making it easy for us to detect them. We didn't ever want to be compromised.

At nighttime, for example, I would have the watch from 11 to 12. The guy next to me would have 12 to 1, the guy next to him, etc. At least one of us was awake 24/7. If the person on guard duty heard something unusual, dangerous, or potentially threatening, the person on guard would wake all of us by softly saying, "Hey, I just heard something. Did you hear something? Can you see something?"

During the night, our higher headquarters would call us every hour. They usually have three to six teams out there. Our team was 1-2. They would call us up and say "Team 1-2. Team 1-2. Team 1-2. If your situation is negative, break squelch twice." We would press the "push to talk" button on the hand receiver of our PRC-77 radios, so we wouldn't have to talk. They knew that we were okay. That was our SOP.

If we missed three consecutive situation reports, then they figured the worst. They would anticipate we had been either killed or captured. They would send a reaction team to our last known location.

That was a day's work for us. We worked as a team.

## Trust Is Earned

When I was in Vietnam, we'd go on patrol with former North Vietnamese Army (NVA) soldiers who had defected. We called them Kit Carson Scouts.

They all went through a vetting process, but we didn't trust them at first. But we had to use them.

We were operating in their backyard. That's where they lived. They were in the jungle all the time. This was their whole world. They sometimes spent years of their lives in the jungle.

We didn't trust them for a minute. We were always on super high alert with those guys. But I remember one occasion when we heard rustling in the bushes. Our initial thought is that the enemy has spotted us. It put us all on edge because it was a noise we were unfamiliar with.

You can't see more than five or six feet ahead of you in the triple-canopy jungle.

We got our rifles up.

We watched our Kid Carson Scout.

He didn't speak good English. As I said, we can't talk in the jungle. We use hand and arm signals.

We're thinking the NVA are coming closer to us, and they are probing the nearby jungle to locate us and kill or capture us.

But our Kit Carson Scout listened closely, and he indicated the sound was a deer or a small animal near us making noise. He said it must have been upwind of us because if the deer had smelled us, the animal would have taken off lickety-split.

They're aware of those kinds of noises because they live there.

We built respect for him, knowing that he could determine different kinds of noises in the jungle.

You need to learn to trust your teammates. And that trust has to be earned.

## The Biggest Lessons I Learned

Teamwork matters. You're not there just for your safety. You're there for the safety of your buddy next to you too. You go in as a team. You come out as a team. You work together as a team. If the team succeeds, you succeed.

You lose friends along the way through combat, sickness, or illness. But the core team, four or five members, stays together. They rotate in. Teamwork is the core.

Knowing your strengths and weaknesses and your buddy's strengths and weaknesses is crucial.

Knowing your motivation and drive—why are you doing this? You're doing it for the unit and supporting the unit and the mission.

Those are the important lessons.

## Questions to Educate, Empower, and Inspire

- Does your team act as a team?
- What have they done to show you they are a team?
- What can be improved?
- How will you help them improve as a team?

Headquarters
Multi-National Force – Iraq
APO AE 09342-1400

September 1, 2008

To the Soldiers of the 300th Military Police Brigade:

As you prepare to redeploy, please accept my heartfelt thanks for your dedicated service and outstanding performance. In your superior execution of detainee operations for Multi-National Force-Iraq, you have had a dramatic impact on the security progress in Iraq. Congratulations on a job well-done!

Your success in employing "COIN inside the wire" practices has had an enormous impact on our overall mission. You have skillfully implemented reconciliation programs, conducting over 12,000 MNFRC boards and providing literacy, religious, and civics education to thousands of detainees. First at Camp Bucca and then at Camp Cropper, you upgraded facilities, increased opportunities for family members to visit, and coordinated thousands of detainee movements. It is no small task to run the largest and busiest military detention facilities in the world, and you have done so with admirable skill and professionalism. Your efforts have resulted in unprecedented high standards and in over 8,000 detainees being released, better prepared to resist extremist propaganda and to engage in civic life.

Your impressive implementation of COIN principles has extended beyond detention operations. You have organized numerous medical outreach engagements, CERP projects, and clothing drives to better the lives of the Iraqi people. And by training and partnering with over 1,500 Iraqi Corrections Officers, you have better prepared Iraq to run its own detention operations and foster reconciliation.

Through all of your efforts, you have helped to advance the strategic interests of the United States and to provide hope and a better future for the Iraqi people. You should be immensely proud. Thank you, and well done!

With gratitude,

Well done!

David H. Petraeus
General, United States Army
Commanding

I was honored to have served with such dedicated and professional Soldiers from Brigade, Battalion, Company, and Detachment level during our tour of duty in Iraq during "The Surge" (2007-2008), culminating in receiving this "Thanks for a Job Well" done letter to the Soldiers of the 300th Military Police Brigade.

# Chapter 12
# Dealing with Adversity

Our six-man, Special Forces team had successfully parachuted from our green Huey helicopter in our drop zone at Camp Pendleton about 38 miles from downtown San Diego in 1978. We looked up in the sky for the next group of six jumpers to exit their bird.

Six men jumped out. But we counted only five open parachutes.

We saw that the last jumper had exited the aircraft, but his parachute didn't open.

This was a scary moment for us.

We were making static line jumps. Static line main parachutes are designed with 18 feet of static line. You hook up your static line to the anchor point. In this case, it was a wire cable arrayed in a doughnut ring circle attached to the helicopter's floor. When you jump out and get to the end of the static line, your chute opens automatically.

Later, we learned that the wire that circles the aircraft's floor had pulled apart, so his static line never stayed attached to the helicopter. We typically jump at 1,250 feet AGL (adjusted ground level) and have a terminal velocity of 120 miles per hour. When the static line malfunctions, you've got one or two seconds to make up your mind to pull your reserve chute, or it will be too late. Your parachute needs four seconds to open normally.

This jumper's name was Major Charles A. Peak. He was the commander of the Special Forces unit.

We watched him stream down. His main chute never opened. He deployed his reserve at the last second, and it barely had time to fill with air. He had even less time to react because he landed on the side of the hill, not in a valley. That was a blessing because he could absorb the impact by landing on the side of the canyon hillside and then rolling down the hill. We ran over to make sure he was okay. Miraculously, he didn't break any bones. If he had landed on a canyon valley floor, he would have broken many bones and might not have lived. He was a little shaken up. We were happy to see that he was still alive and in one piece.

How did he not break any bones? When you do a parachute landing fall, you are trained to keep your feet and knees together. You land with both feet all the time and either lean forward, backward, or sideways. That is built into your muscle memory. So when he landed on the side of the hill, he skidded down the mountain. It was steep enough that he didn't hit solid ground. It broke his fall.

We have a rule when something like that happens. It's like getting bucked off a horse. You need to get right back on. We found that nine times out of 10 if someone has a mishap in a parachute jump, he will lose his confidence and will never want to jump again. He must go back up immediately and jump again. He has to get his confidence back right away, or he'll say, "I'm not jumping anymore. I'm taking myself off jump status. This is too risky for me. I need to work at a desk."

He was the boss. He was the commander. We told him, "Sir, you need to get a fresh parachute back on and get back on that aircraft and jump again."

We convinced him that he needed to go back up there. It took about an hour. We had five other guys with him. He was the first one to jump out of the plane. He landed successfully.

He overcame that near-fatal parachute jump. He turned the situation around. Instead of being afraid, he got back in another aircraft, and he jumped about two hours later and regained his confidence in himself and his equipment.

Adversity enters every person's life. It is up to the individual, the team, and the leader to help each other overcome fears and failures.

## Taps

Unfortunately, this story has a sad ending.

We called Charles A. Peak "Cap" because he was a captain in the Green Berets, and his initials were C.A.P. He was exposed to Agent Orange in Vietnam and developed cancer. He was undergoing chemotherapy to stop the devastating effects of the cancer.

My Army buddies and I visited him in the hospital during his recovery from chemo. He was drained. Before that cancer, he was a very strong guy, but chemotherapy takes a lot out of you. He was weak. So we tried to pep him up.

While he was in the hospital undergoing chemotherapy, tragedy struck his family.

He lived in Tierrasanta, which is northeast of downtown San Diego. Tierrasanta had been a bombing range for the Navy Aircraft stationed at Miramar Naval Air Station. They used to shoot rockets and artillery into Tierrasanta. The builders were supposed to have sterilized the land and made sure there weren't any unexploded ordnance. But a few weeks before Christmas, his two sons and a neighbor were playing in the canyon behind their house. They found unexploded ordnance. They didn't know what it was. The kids were playing with the unexploded device and exploded. His son and the next-door neighbor's son died. His other son was injured.

His wife was devastated. She went to the hospital and told Cap the bad news.

He was overwhelmed, exhausted, and depressed with all that bad news. He was too weak from the recent chemotherapy. The next day, he passed away to be with his son in Heaven.

Here's a guy who had earned his Green Beret as a Special Forces Officer and was Ranger qualified. I found out later that Cap was a Ranger Training officer when I attended Ranger School in 1969. And he served in combat in Vietnam with the 5th Special Forces Group. He served his country, his community (as a Deputy District Attorney), and his family with honor.

In January, we went to his funeral and celebration of life. They had a flyover of helicopters in a missing man formation, a bagpiper, and many speeches. It was devastating that we lost a very good man, Charles A. Peak. RIP.

## Questions to Educate, Empower, and Inspire

- How do you deal with adversity?
- Does this method help you or hurt you?
- What can you do to improve how you deal with adversity?

# Chapter 13
# Grace

As in most organizations, the Army has tiers of leadership. People at all levels make decisions. If they can't decide, they pass the problem up the tier. It's like a pyramid. When things got to my level, the situation usually involved a significant decision.

As the General in charge of Camp Bucca, I was responsible for everything, including the care, comfort, and safety of the detainees, our troops, and our military contractors, including our translators, custodians, and any local nationals working on the base. I needed to enforce all our orders to ensure everyone's safety.

That included General Order Number One, which prohibits soldiers from having alcohol in a combat zone.

The contractors can have alcohol in their huts, but they can't consume it in front of troops. We don't sell alcohol on the base, so contractors must go off base and get alcohol from the locals, which is hard to do in a Muslim country because the locals didn't drink alcohol. Nevertheless, the contractors did find alcohol.

It came to my attention that three female soldiers were accused of drinking vodka provided by a contractor. He tried to seduce these three females with a bottle of vodka. They went to his hut, talked, and drank alcohol. They took the bottle of vodka. After they finished drinking, they threw the bottle into a dumpster.

The JAG officer told me, "We've got signed reports and affidavits by soldiers and officers who smelled alcohol on their breaths. The women denied they drank."

The women came into me one at a time to plead their cases. One of the females had pictures she had sent to her friends back home. She was holding this bottle of vodka. She told me, "Sir, there was no vodka in there. We just filled it up with water. And we were trying to boast to our friends back home that we're having a good time."

I did not believe they were drinking water because of the many signed affidavits. So I gave them a General Officer Memorandum of Reprimand. A GOMOR is a letter of reprimand given to a soldier by a General Officer (GCMCA). A General Officer Letter of Reprimand can be filed in either a Soldier's Official Military Personnel File ("permanent file") or their Military Personnel Record Jacket ("local file"). This is serious because a reprimand would most likely prevent a person from getting promoted. Typically, a GOMOR is a career-killer for the soldier—as it is often meant to be. The GOMOR follows the soldier indefinitely (which means promotion boards see it) unless filed only locally.

One of the women was a major. About five years later, she wrote to me and told me she couldn't get promoted because of the GOMOR in her file. She said, "I've been a model officer. Would you consider taking it out of my permanent record?"

I looked at the documentation she sent. I talked to a few people to ensure her documents were valid, and she hadn't made it up. After about a week, I decided to say, "Yes, okay. I'll take the GOMOR out of your permanent record."

She got promoted to Lieutenant Colonel because she learned her lesson.

She violated the general order, but she took the reprimand to heart, and she realized that if you wanted to stay in the military and move forward, you would have to be a model soldier and a model officer.

Leaders need to realize that people can and should learn from their mistakes. No one is perfect, and no one does the right thing all the time. However, if people acknowledge their errors and want to move forward, they should be given a second chance.

I realized this because I was given a second chance.

## My Second Chance

In 1970, when I was in Vietnam, alcohol was used as a morale booster. They gave us two cans of beer a day to keep up morale. The people in my unit primarily drank beer. But some people smoked pot and used recreational drugs, which violated the Uniform Code of Military Justice (UCMJ).

We would go to the nearby mess hall and have evening chow at dinner. Then after dark, we'd show up at the little Quonset hut in our company area, designated as the Morale Welfare and Recreation (MWR) hut. We'd have a free beer or two and tell each other war stories, usually of our last mission. Some soldiers would peel off, go down to a couple of Quonset huts, and smoke their marijuana or do other recreational drugs. I never went near them. I stayed with my buddies and drank a few more beers. Rumors were going around that some recreational drugs were laced with rat poison to kill unsuspecting GIs.

One soldier in our unit advertised for guys who had illicit drugs and smoke marijuana. Eventually, our leadership transferred him out of our unit and told him never to return to our company area.

But he came back about once a week and met his old buddies to smoke marijuana and do illegal stuff.

Our first sergeant came into our team and said, "Hey, if he comes back here, I want you guys to remind him that he should never come back here and that he is not welcome here. Do you understand what I'm telling you?"

We said, "Okay, first sergeant."

A couple of nights later, he came back. My Team Leader said, "Okay, we will give this guy a blanket party to make sure he knows never to come back here."

Six of us encircled him. His friends saw us coming. They took off.

The guy next to me said to the pot smoker, "Hey, you're not supposed to be back here. You were told to get the f**k out here. I don't want you ever coming back here again."

The guy shrugged his shoulders and said, "Okay, I'll leave."

My guy said, "Oh, no, you're not getting off that easy."

Someone threw a blanket over his head. We just punched him a few times. We didn't tear him up. He fell to the ground, and we walked away.

He reported the incident to his leadership and pressed charges. The Criminal Investigation Division (CID) talked with our leadership, and they interviewed each of us one at a time.

As a result, we all received a company-level Article 15, which meant the report went into our temporary records as a derogatory comment. The company commander docked us a week's pay, which for me as an E5 was $79. He also put us on restricted duty so we could not leave the company area. We had nowhere to go anyway. We had to do chores like picking up cigarette butts, cleaning the company area, and painting rocks white. We did not have flush toilets. We used 55-gallon drums cut in half with a piece of wood over the top with a hole cut in the middle to poop into. We had to add diesel fuel to the buckets, light it on fire, and stir the human poop until it burned up.

But the company commander said this reprimand was a company-level Article 15 that wouldn't go into our permanent records, which would have ended my career. Instead, he said it would be in our temporary folders. If I didn't do anything else wrong while I was in Vietnam, this temporary folder would be burned before I left Vietnam.

We thought we would never see that Article 15 again.

However, it did stay in my permanent file and showed up later. That incident was a big mistake on my part, and I was sorry I ever was involved and vowed to myself that I would never again do something stupid like that.

I learned my lesson like the Major I mentioned in the alcohol story. I maintained a stellar career after that. I did not do anything that was considered conduct unbecoming or even close. So even though I had a blemish on my record, I was able to continue to get promoted up to general.

## Questions to Educate, Empower, and Inspire

- Have you ever done something you regretted? How did you atone for that mistake?
- Did that mistake cost hurt your career?
- What would you do if one of your direct reports made a serious mistake?

# Chapter 14
# Motivation

If I asked you to sleep less than four hours a night and eat only one meal a day, could you do it?

Your first thought probably would be a resounding, "No way."

But you'd be surprised by what your body can do.

Our bodies can do much more than most people ever thought.

Combat takes a toll on your body and your mind. The lack of sleep and food is a fact of life in the military. However, people train for that. The military conducts training that enhances your physical endurance and pushes your body to many extremes to prepare for every situation.

Your body can take it for the most part, unless you get to your failure point.

When I was in Ranger School, we had very little time for sleep and not enough food. You never knew when your next meal would come. We might get one meal one day, two meals the next, and none the following day. We walked with weapons and combat loaded the equivalent of 200 miles in two months. We were up most of the night. Those situations prepared us for combat.

From my experiences in Vietnam, Iraq, and Afghanistan, I know that the higher you are in rank, typically the less sleep you get at night. When they're in a combat situation, generals usually sleep less than four hours a night. That's a demand you put on your body because you need the time, focus, and attention to do many duties, tasks, and functions.

You can train your body to do superhuman things.

When the war in Iraq first kicked off in 2003, I worked on a general's staff. General Stan McChrystal slept less than four hours a night. He ate only one meal a day. A *Rolling Stone* reporter attached to McChrystal and shadowed him for six weeks solid. He said he saw the general eat only twice in those six weeks.

McChrystal was a high-energy person. He was motivated. He was self-driven. He was responsible for a lot of men's and women's lives. He took his job seriously.

He'd go to bed at one o'clock in the morning. He'd be back in the office by four o'clock in the morning at the latest. He did this for at least six months straight.

If the situation demands it and you need to perform at that level, you can do that indefinitely.

Stan McChrystal was both an Army Ranger and Special Forces Officer before becoming a General. The Army pushes you to your physical extremes and your mental extremes. As you move up in the military, like in the civilian world, you have more responsibility and more things that you're responsible for, so the expectations are higher.

If you can't meet each level's requirements, you don't get promoted because your peers do. They move up without you.

Of course, the same is true in your life, although not to the extreme I mentioned in the military.

You do not need to live on four hours of sleep or eat only one meal a day. But it would help if you stayed fit, ate well, slept well, and took care of your body, so you perform at your best. If your life is out of balance, your actions and thinking can be out of balance. So, if you are packing a few extra pounds or wondering when you can find time to exercise, remember the example of the people in the military who have endured so much more.

Remember, your body can do more than you think it can.

## Questions to Educate, Empower, and Inspire

- What motivates you?
- What de-motivates you?
- What can you do to increase your motivation?

# Chapter 15
# Discipline

During the early stages of the Iraq War, members of the United States Army and the CIA committed a series of human rights violations and war crimes against detainees in the Abu Ghraib prison in Iraq.

U.S. Defense Secretary, Donald Rumsfeld, reportedly initiated pressure on troops at Abu Ghraib to obtain "actionable intelligence." As a result of this, abuses at Abu Ghraib occurred.

To refresh your memory, several officers and soldiers were removed from duty, court-martialed, sentenced to prison, or dishonorably discharged.

A reserve component MP unit guarded the Abu Ghraib prison out of New York. They were all but forgotten about, so it was kind of like living on an island of 280 acres surrounded by hostiles and aggressive insurgents. Under the U.S. MP Doctrine, detainee facilities are supposed to be in a secure rear area to be guarded and supported logistically. The Abu

Ghraib violations happened because a reserve component MP unit did not have the dynamic leadership and experience needed to stand up to the pressure.

It takes many years to get to the proper level of training and experience. They were called up six months before the war started. The military extended their stay in Iraq for another 90 days, and their morale went south. The leadership wasn't up to speed to handle the mission.

We had 150,000 troops on the ground at the peak of the second Iraq war (OIF). And 53% of the soldiers were reserve components. They were under constant threat and exposed to enemy attacks almost daily.

Abu was a hotbed for the insurgency. It's within 20-to-thirty minutes from Ramadi and Fallujah (main battlegrounds).

The enemy would attack almost every day. They would lob mortars into the 40-acre complex surrounded by high walls. They used artillery rounds on occasion. And randomly, they would make a combined attack by crashing a suicide driver with an IED into the outer wall and then attack us with a dismounted ground attack.

In one fierce attack in early April 2005, at least 20 U.S. soldiers and 12 detainees were wounded when 40 to 60 insurgents attacked the infamous Abu Ghraib.

Well, the personnel wasn't trained for external protection. An MP unit is trained for internal protection and securing the detainees and prisoners of war.

Like any war, the enemy looks for weakness and tries to exploit it. In that situation, there weren't enough ground forces on the outside to protect the environment entirely. We had gone into Operation Iraqi Freedom with fewer troops than we usually would have.

I visited Abu Ghraib many times to check on things. I was the Provost Marshall for all of Iraq during that period. I kept advising my generals that they needed to get out there, make a site visit and provide these guys with more support and logistical resources. And it was a hellhole out there. But the general told me, "Hey, Bob, there are many hellholes in Iraq. So, we'll deal with that when we come to it."

As a leader, you need to ensure your team has the proper training and resources to deal with any situation. As the leader, you are responsible. As they say, "The buck stops here." If you do not provide proper leadership, the consequences could be disastrous for you, your company, and even your family. In the case of Abu Ghraib, several officers were sentenced to prison and served time for these actions.

## Questions to Educate, Empower, and Inspire

- Have you been in a situation where discipline was called for and met the challenge?
- What helped you get through that situation?
- How can you prepare for difficult situations?

# Chapter 16
# Be Prepared

My most exhilarating memory from being in the Army was flying into a landing zone in a helicopter. You never knew whether the enemy would surround that landing zone. It was always an unknown, and you had to stay vigilant.

In the early 80s, I was Executive Officer on a twelve-man Special Forces team, and we were working in the Republic of South Korea. We call them RoKs—Republic of Korea Special Forces Team. We spent five days preparing and getting ready. We learned about the terrain and our mission.

Around midnight, 12 of us Green Berets jumped at 1,500 feet out of the C 123 aircraft.

However, the Korean pilots put us out in the wrong location, over a river.

As were descended, we worried that we could drown if we landed in the water. Fortunately, we didn't land in the river, but we had problems. The team commander broke his ankle on impact. One guy twisted his ankle. Another guy hurt his back.

So three guys were out of the mission.

We usually have support people on the ground near the drop zone for events like that.

But since we dropped in the wrong location, the support team took about 40 minutes to reach the area to evacuate those guys.

There was a vast difference between being in that noisy aircraft and being on the ground. Suddenly, you're trying to be as quiet as possible and then move out of the area so the enemy can't find us.

The Koreans wanted to move overnight to a new location about 20 miles away.

We were solid and competent. We trained for this. We were prepared. But we were not prepared to move 20 miles at night, in the dark, and try to be quiet and not be noticed by the villagers. When we walked through the villages, the dogs barked.

We finished that mission, and we got reunited with the three injured men.

That was a successful mission. We used our strengths and tenacity to accomplish the mission.

There's a funny ending to this story.

The guy who twisted his ankle landed in a pigpen! The pigs tried to eat him alive!

Remember, he was weighed down by a 100-pound backpack and his parachute gear. He had to fight his way out, so he didn't get eaten alive.

You really do need to be prepared for anything!

## Preparing for Anything

When I was serving in Vietnam in 1970, we were told that Vietnam War protesters who worked in an ordinance factory sabotaged M-67 "baseball" hand grenades.

Hand grenades are designed to explode after a five-to-eight-second delay after pulling the pin and letting the handle flip up. We were taught to pull the pin, let the handle fly, and count to three seconds before throwing the grenade. You don't want to throw it too quickly because the enemy might have enough time to pick up your grenade and throw it back at you.

In this ordinance factory, the protestors manipulated the composition of the hand grenades so that when you pulled the pin, the grenade will explode instantaneously.

Soon after this became known, an urgent directive came down from higher command to all units in Vietnam. They had identified the lot numbers and serial numbers of the fatally flawed hand grenades. Hand grenades are shipped in wooden boxes which are identified with lot numbers and serial numbers. We checked our inventory to see if we had been issued any of those fatally flawed hand grenades.

Fortunately, we didn't have those. But U.S. workers were willing to kill U.S. troops. This negatively impacted our morale. We were very fortunate that none of our troops were killed by M-67 hand grenades.

## Questions to Educate, Empower, and Inspire

- Are you prepared for anything that could happen to your company?
- Are you prepared for anything that could happen to yourself or your family?
- What one step can you take now to become more prepared?

# Chapter 17
# Completing the Mission: Lead Like a General

When I think about generals who inspired me, I don't necessarily think of the dramatic people who led the charge into battle. The Army's mission is more than just fighting wars. It is about consistency, the ability to execute plans, lead people, and be role models for others to follow. Those generals are perfect examples of loyalty, self-service, duty, and other Army values.

Most Army life is business as usual, going forward, accomplishing the mission, and looking after your team.

Using that criteria, I think of Major General Craig Bambrough as a general who inspired me.

Here's a story that exemplifies the teamwork I saw in Major General Bambrough.

Major General Bambrough was the second-highest officer in the Army Reserve. He was in charge of about 200,000 people.

The only person higher in rank was the Chief of the Army Reserve (CAR), who was usually in Washington and worked on the political side. General Bambrough's main job as the deputy commander was twofold: to provide fully trained and fully equipped soldiers ready to be integrated into the Active Army and successfully support the Active Army's mission.

I first met Major General Bambrough when he was a one-star general, and I was assigned to the 221st Military Police (MP) Brigade, which was stationed on Heading Street, San Jose. It was a Federal Army Reserve facility in San Jose across from the San Jose police station.

After a couple of months, he called me into the office and said, "Bob, I see you've got some potential. I think you would be happy in a career being a military police officer."

I said, "Yeah, I'm excited to be a military police officer." One reason for this was that there were fewer and fewer positions for higher-ranking officers. In Special Forces, Captains command the Operational Detachments or "A" Teams. They spend most of their time in the field and are called "Air Borne Commandos." "B" Teams are usually "Chair Borne Commandos" and rarely operate in the field.

My career took off because he believed in me. And ultimately, I had the honor to be promoted to Brigadier General. I had Saddam Hussein in one of our detention facilities along with other High-Value Detainees (HVDs). They were featured in the card deck of the 55 Most Wanted Iraqis.

The Defense Intelligence Agency developed a set of 55 playing cards to help troops identify the most-wanted members of President Saddam Hussein's government. Some of them included Hussein's family members, like his sons Uday and Qusay. I was the Commanding General of Camp Bucca, which at that time was the largest detention facility in Iraq with more than 20,000 detainees, 5,000 troops, and thousands of contractors. Because of Major General Bambrough, you could say I had a pretty exciting life.

Major General Bambrough was initially an artillery officer. He was a good leader, an inspirational leader, and most of all, very humble.

When he served in Vietnam as a Lieutenant, he was awarded two Silver Stars for his heroic actions in combat. You only get a Silver Star when you are in a battle where you're engaging the enemy up close and personal. Getting a Silver Star in the military is very rare. The only combat award higher than the Silver Star is the Medal of Honor. And he was awarded two Silver Stars.

I worked closely with him for five years. And he never ever bragged about that.

He never even told war stories about how he got them in Vietnam.

When people prodded him and asked him questions, he gave a little bit of information over time, but he never bragged about how he got those two Silver Stars.

Also, Major General Bambrough coached, taught, and mentored younger officers.

Almost always, on an Army Reserve weekend, he would have an "ODP" session which stood for Officer Development Program. He would bring us into a conference room and talk to us about how to lead by example and how to inspire our troops.

Unlike some generals, he was accessible to people below him. Usually, the chain of command is very inflexible in the military. Rarely would a person several ranks below a general get a chance to speak to a general. But Major General Bambrough made time for people of all ranks. Of course, generals are very busy. But I remember many times when I'd ask to speak to him. He would always tell me when he was available.

He gave me insights into things I did not know.

For example, when I got promoted to Lieutenant Colonel, two ranks below general, he told me to apply immediately for the Army War College (AWC) because completing the AWC or the equivalent service college is the only way to become a general.

There is a short window of opportunity to do the training necessary to be considered for promotion. If he hadn't told me to apply early, I might have missed that window.

He also gave me advice about certain things that we do or don't do in the military.

He helped me a lot. He groomed me. He didn't favor me. He told me what I needed to do, and I picked up on that.

He was an excellent mentor. If not for his advice, I probably would not have had the career I had.

Have you ever considered the impact you make on your direct reports? A bit of advice you share or a door you open for those below you can change their lives.

Major General Bambrough embodied all the army values. He had integrity. Major General Bambrough was always in top physical condition, which inspired his troops to be in shape.

I worked with him for about seven years. Soon after 9/11, he was mobilized full-time and stationed at Fort McPherson, GA, the Command Headquarters of the United States Army Reserve Command (USARC). During a phone call, he asked me to come on active duty to assist him in helping call up and activate Army Reserve Units to support and supplement the Active Army mission. After talking with my wife, I volunteered and went on Temporary Active Duty and was stationed at Fort McPherson, GA. So, starting early December 2001, I saw him day in and day out and attended many daily meetings with him. He sent me to attend many daily meetings at FORSCOM HQs (Forces Command) when he was not available to attend. Every time I saw him, I was inspired to do my job better. His entire work ethic inspired me to be the best I can be.

## Questions to Educate, Empower, and Inspire

- Have you had a leader who inspired you in this manner?
- Do you conduct yourself in a way that inspires your direct reports?

# Chapter 18
# Service: Giving Back to Your Community

Giving back to your community is a great way to attain personal inspiration and stimulate people in your community. One of the most rewarding parts of my current life is coordinating the Placer Veterans Stand Down, a free, two-day event that provides services to vulnerable veterans and their immediate families. We provide three meals each day, including delicious desserts. We offer medical, vision, hearing, and dental services.

The most needed service is dental, which the VA doesn't offer unless you're 100% disabled. We had 16 dentists help veterans clean, drill, fill, and get their teeth up to date.

We also provided career counseling services, housing referrals, and VA benefits assistance. We also gave free clothing and personal care supplies. Vets could also get a haircut and take a shower. Local veterinarians took care of pets who needed vaccinations and supplies, all thanks to the Banfield Foundation.

In 2020, about 400 Veterans and their immediate family members came. We did not host a Stand Down in 2021 because of COVID.

I am honored and blessed to be the President/CEO of the Placer Veterans Stand Down (PVSD). It's a major planning effort to get all those resources. It's kind of like herding cats sometimes because all the services are provided by volunteers.

I am on the board of six veteran service organizations, and I support several others. I have a lifelong passion for helping veterans because they have given so much to our country.

I have a little saying that I share with most of the veterans' groups I speak to, "When you look at yourself in the morning, you can know that you've given more to your country than you will ever take back."

Less than 1% of our population of 350 million people are in the military—less than two million people are on active or reserve component military.

They have given a lot to us. They and their families have paid a price. Many soldiers were killed and didn't come back. They left families behind. They left their wives behind.

I'm at a point in my life where I have the ability and drive to help people by giving back to people in my community who might not have had the advantages and experiences I had.

Sharing my experiences can help and support those people.

## Questions to Educate, Empower, and Inspire

- How could you give back to your community?
- Is there a way for your company to participate in a community enrichment program?
- Are you willing to spearhead this effort?

# Chapter 19
# Lessons for Success

I'd like to tell you the story of a soldier named Greg who worked in the same office space as me at Camp Victory, Iraq, in 2003 when things were hot and heavy.

At that time in Iraq, we had first-generation Humvees. The High Mobility Multipurpose Wheeled Vehicles (HMMWV; colloquial: Humvee) are a family of light, four-wheel drive military trucks and utility vehicles. They didn't provide much protection. They had canvas sides, no overhead cover, and plastic windows. They did not have body armor.

One day while driving out of the guarded Forward Operating Base (FOB), Greg was sitting in the passenger seat of his Humvee. At a stop sign, he looked to the right, then looked straight ahead. And at that split second, a 7.62 mm, AK-47 bullet pierced his right cheek and gouged a tunnel across his cheek. The bullet probably would have killed him if he had been looking to the right a second before.

He had a big, dark scar across his face. We called it a "dueling scar" because it looked like a scar from a sword or a knife.

He went to the hospital to get stitched up and checked out. He was shaken up but he was okay. It was a sympathy scar.

The bullet that pierced his skin went through the front windshield shield leaving a clean hole with a few spider cracks. Later, Greg went to the motor pool and asked if he could keep the broken windshield and ship it home. Later, he made a coffee table out of it. He used the broken windshield as a war souvenir and conversation starter.

Greg was an Army Reservist and would be returning to civilian life when he returned home. He told me he was running for office in Kentucky, and his facial scar would give him some sympathy and support.

The moral of the story is that when life gives you lemons, you can make lemonade.

## Challenge Yourself Every Day

Many motivational speakers have said you should do at least one challenging or difficult thing every day.

My outdoor swimming pool in Northern California is not heated. In the winter, the temperature gets down to about 49 degrees. Every day, I dive into the cold water of the pool and swim two laps.

It was a challenge for me. I knew that I had the discipline and the willpower to do it. The ritual was cleansing, purifying, and a test of my willpower.

But sometimes, I had to talk to myself and convince myself that I needed to jump in the pool. I knew that if I could jump into the cold water and swim two laps, I could do an hour of cold calling later to help my wife generate new leads for our real estate business. I did that diving for dollars routine for three and a half years until I caught some upper respiratory issues, and I didn't want to extend medical issues.

I used to work out at my local gym regularly, but COVID changed everything. Now I do the X3 workout program at home about six days a week. It's very strenuous. It's a short (about 10 minutes) but intense muscle-building workout. That's what I want at this point in my life.

The X3 is a complete home gym system that provides faster, better exercise benefits through variable resistance training. It uses a metal ground plate, heavy-duty elastic tubing (strongly reinforced bands), and a long steel bar with grips to hold the bands. This system allows you to perform various exercises to increase muscle mass, strength, and bone density.

I supplement my strength training with X3 resistance bands and by hitting the golf course for physical and social activity. I also go mountain bike riding. My running days are over because of my bad knees (and I've had my right knee replaced three times). And as of this week, I am still in rehab recovering from my third knee replacement. I guess they don't make them like they used to.

I learned that President George W. Bush had given up jogging because of his bad knees and ran several miles a day when he was the President. He underwent knee surgery and had both knees replaced in May 2014 and afterward started his avid mountain biking on bike trails on his Texas ranch.

My advice is that if you want to live a long, strong, and prosperous life, you should keep active every day doing something you are enthusiastic about and do something that's challenging to you. Do not take the easy road.

## Fill Your Head with Positive Thoughts Before Going to Sleep

My wife and I started watching the TV series, *Heartland,* a few years ago. It's very entertaining. It's a multigenerational love story wrapped around horses and the spectacular outdoor scenery of Calgary, Canada. My wife and I are into horses. We have a small working ranch with a couple of horses.

*Heartland* is very wholesome. There are no swear words, smoking, or vivid sex scenes. And what would a love story be without some enthusiastic kissing scenes? It's addictive, and fun to watch. We binged three episodes the other night.

I like to watch something wholesome and nourishing before I go to bed rather than watching the late-night news. Most nights, if we put on the 11 o'clock news, we do not see any good stories. I do not want to go to bed after watching bad news stories reported near me or somewhere else in the world. I'd rather watch something like *Heartland*, which has happy endings most of the time.

## Help When You Can

Ranger John and I served in Vietnam together in 1970 with L Company 75th Ranger, 101st Airborne Division at Camp Eagle. John was assigned to a different six-man Long Range Reconnaissance Team (LRRP). Still, we had similar experiences until he was wounded in combat twice, and he was evacuated to the Army Hospital in Japan for care and rehab before returning to Vietnam. Ever since returning from his tours of duty in Vietnam, he's had a hard time keeping a job.

John told me about a recurring nightmare he had. He was in a two-day firefight with the large NVA force. His unit was almost overrun. But they repelled the enemy, and the NVA finally retreated into the jungle. On the evening of the second day, Medivac helicopters evacuated the wounded and dead. John was wounded by shrapnel, patched up and stabilized, and ready to be evacuated. Since his wounds were not as bad as some of his buddies, he was on the last Medivac bird out. He boarded the Medivac along with seven or eight bodies of those KIA. The bodies were not covered with tarps. Fresh blood dripped on the helicopter's floor. John sat on the outside of the bird, looking at the faces of the recent KIA soldiers. As the bird lifted off, it was getting darker outside, and the flashing red navigation lights blinked off and on. It was about an hour's flight to the Medivac LZ, and John kept seeing the eerie sight of dead bloody faces flashing back at him. This death ride took place over 50 years ago, and scenes from that night still haunt John.

He's got PTSD. His condition is nothing crazy, but he doesn't get along well with most people.

Since he was emotionally disabled and couldn't keep a job, he fought and fought with the VA to get his disability approved. After more than 20 years, he was finally approved for 70% disability. Since he could not keep a job, he applied for VA Unemployability. A few more years went by, and the VA finally agreed. Now he is considered 100% disabled, and he receives a monthly disability payment. One of the most important benefits of 100% disability is that you are eligible for Dental Benefits from the VA which is one of the most requested services.

John used some of his disability money to buy a Prius about 20 years ago. He still lives in his Prius.

I said, "John, you're getting full disability from the VA now. You should be able to afford to rent an apartment or even buy a small house."

"I can't really, Bob."

"Why, John?"

"Well, part of my PTSD is I that am a hoarder."

"What do you mean?"

"I put stuff into storage. I've got six storage containers full of stuff that I pay rent for storage."

That eats up most of his disability check.

"John, I could drive down there to your location, and we could go through that stuff and get rid of a lot of it."

"Oh, no, Bob, I can't do that."

So, here's a single guy (never married) with no kids. He is a decorated Vietnam Combat War Veteran awarded two Purple Hearts who has had multiple tours in Vietnam and cannot reconnect to regular society. Among other things, hoarding is a symptom of PTSD.

I want to help him because we need to help our buddies on and off the battlefield long after the battle has ended, even after 50 years. But sometimes your advice or help goes by the wayside as the other person doesn't want help or is stuck in their emotions and won't change their situation for the better. You have to move on knowing you tried your best to help.

## Capture Your Ideas

I worked for a startup company. One day, we were riding in the elevator when the CEO turned to us, the only employees, and said, "Remember this day. There's only six of us now, but we're going to grow and expand, and one day, we'll be in the Fortune 500." We all had founders' stock, and we all thought we'd get a good return for efforts down the road.

That resonated with me.

This was about a year before 9/11 happened, and we were on our second or third round of venture capital money. After 9/11 started, I got called to duty. About five years later, I checked in with him. Unfortunately, the company went sideways and fizzled out. They ran out of venture capital money and never got off the ground.

I have learned that there are many unsuccessful companies for every successful company in Silicon Valley. This one wasn't that successful. Stuff happens.

But it's a good story of optimism, vision, and leadership. The boss was a high-energy, very dynamic guy. He inspired me to think differently.

I'd like to make another point.

One day, I was in his office, and I said to him, "Many people wake up in the middle of the night and think of an idea. They write it on a notepad. But I'll bet you have a big whiteboard in your bedroom. And when you get up in the middle of the night, you write something down that just came to your mind, and you go back to bed."

He said, "That's amazing, Bob. How did you know that? I do have a whiteboard in my bedroom. My wife gets upset at me sometimes when I jump out of bed and write something on my whiteboard and then go back to bed because I want to keep that thought and develop it tomorrow."

I do not necessarily wake up in the middle of the night with a new idea. But for me, the most fruitful and thoughtful time is within a half-hour window of going to bed or when I first wake up in the morning.

I have a routine when I go to bed. I brush my teeth, put my pajamas on, start thinking about things I'm doing tomorrow, what the highlights of today were, and then I put my head on the pillow.

I usually wake up around 5:30 or 6 a.m., and I will be quiet and lay in bed thinking about things.

My inspirational moments are that 15-to-20-minute window before I go to sleep and when I first wake up.

## Find a Way to Relieve Your Anxiety

Here's a funny story...

We had a decisive firefight with the NVA in which none of us were injured or killed. After we returned to our company area later that evening. We were having a few beers in the company day room or club, and then we decided to turn in for the night. We went to our hooches (living quarters: a small room in the Quonset hut). I shared it with my teammate Bob Wimmer.

The company Quonset huts were basically wood structures about 30 feet long. They are reinforced with sandbags stacked four feet high along the sides of the outside perimeter. A corrugated tin roof with a few sandbags was placed on top. There were about five, small rooms on each side of the Quonset hut each divided by plywood walls. The rooms (about 8 feet by 8 feet) were set up with bunk beds for two men to sleep in each room.

We had electricity powered by a generator for lighting. A wire with a hanging light bulb hung in the middle of each room but there were no light switches. So you had to unscrew the light bulb to switch off the light. I was on the top bunk and Wimmer was in the bottom bunk. When we finally got into our bunks, I told Wimmer it was his turn to unscrew the light bulb. He didn't want to burn his hands. He was a little drunk and still feisty, so he pulled out his 1911 pistol and fired a round up through the corrugated roof, hitting and breaking the light bulb.

We both laughed and put our heads on our pillows. Soon afterwards, the First Sergeant opened the door at the end of the building and yelled, "What the f**k was that?"

Wimmer yelled back "It's okay First Sergeant! I just shot out the light bulb."

The First Sergeant, being cautious, decided not to enter the building with a couple of drunk and rowdy soldiers yelled back. "Okay you two f**k knuckles, report to my office first thing in the morning."

He then closed the door and left the area.

The next morning, when we were sober, we reported to his office. He yelled obscenities at us for a good while and asked, "What the f**k were you thinking shooting a gun inside your Quonset hut?"

Wimmer told him, "Sergeant, we were just letting off some steam."

He yelled at us some more, and then he told us to never do that ever again and get to f**k out of his office.

Shenanigans like this happened from time to time but the good news was no one was ever hit by friendly fire.

The moral of that story is that you need to find a positive way to release your anxiety and stress before you do something that you might regret later. Like shoot out a light bulb or smash your fist into a wall.

I like to reduce my stress and anxiety levels by going for an hour mountain bike ride on the country dirt trails near the lake. Before I developed a knee problem, I used to go for hour-long runs three to five times a week.

The two best parts of doing extended cardio like running or biking are (first) you have time to think about what's been bothering you, and (second) you can look at the problem from many different angles without any annoying distractions.

And for most people, including me, you will get another benefit. Runners call it a natural high. And when I do my hour-long, intense mountain bike riding, I feel euphoric as my body releases natural beta-endorphins/opiates. This elevates my mood, and I feel better for the rest of the day.

Endorphins are feel-good chemicals naturally manufactured in the brain when the body experiences extended physical activity, pain, or stress. They are called the natural opiates of the body that are an added physical/emotional bonus or a serendipity effect.

## Questions to Educate, Empower, and Inspire

- When are you most creative?
- How do you capture your ideas?
- How do you decide which ideas to act on?

# Chapter 20
# Leaving a Legacy-Living a Life on Purpose

I came back from Vietnam with PTSD due to survivor guilt. I never got seriously wounded in Vietnam. As an upfront and personnel infantry-type intelligence collector (LRRP), I saw a lot of carnage during and after firefights. And I conducted Battle Damage Assessments (BDA) after B-52 Arclight missions, where the planes usually dropped 500-pound bombs. For example, one of my six-man LRRP team's missions put my team on this hilltop and put another six-man team on another hilltop a couple of miles away. And then, within two days, that other team was killed in a fierce firefight. None of them came back alive.

I think about that. We could have easily been switched. If they put my LRRP team on that hilltop and put them down on our hilltop, then we could have all been killed and not come back.

That was May 11th, 1970. That day still sticks in my mind. Those six young men who never came back alive were my age, my peers. I trained with them and ate in the same mess hall as them. When we were between missions, after work hours, we would enjoy a beer or two and share our experiences of recent field experiences.

So later, when I returned home, I tried to lead my life, knowing that they didn't have the opportunity to move forward with their lives. In a sense, I had survivor guilt. "Why am I still here? What's God's mission for me? Why am I still on the earth?"

I tried to live my life with the knowledge that these six young men hadn't been able to come out of it alive. Those six guys were not able to move forward in their lives. They were not able to have families, have jobs, or contribute to society.

So, I was always trying to do the right thing. Just like in the movie, *Saving Private Ryan*.

My situation is the same scenario. Make *my life* a life worth living. Men have died. Throughout our history and the history of humankind, people have laid down their lives for us so we can live the life that we're now living.

In a sense, I tried to make my life worthy—to pay back for those six young men—and all our fallen heroes.

But because of my training, this ideal is not something you think about. It's not something that I reflect on. It's ingrained in me.

Over time—there are quiet times of your life when you think, "What can I be doing?" For example, getting up at four in the morning and doing physical training. Doing push-ups. Doing five-mile runs before the sun even gets up. Going to school at night. I worked for all my degrees in night school.

When I was in the reserve component, I was in the civilian world. I had a large family. I was involved in my kids' schooling and their activities after school—baseball and scouting. It kept me busy. I'd rather be busy than bored. I went to school two nights a week. When I graduated from school eleven years later, I taught night school two nights a week at the graduate and undergraduate levels for another 10 years.

You internally reflect. It happens in a brief period. And then it is ingrained inside you. You say, "Hey, you know? That could have been me. That could have been us."

I knew I had to keep myself busy. I did not want many downtimes because of the old saying, "An idle mind is the devil's workshop." I tried to keep busy and active, read books, go to school, engage with people, and talk. Just keep busy.

I did have quiet times, of course. I enjoyed getting on my dirt bike and traveling out into the woods. I would shut down my motorcycle, just sit, and reflect on my life… where I'm going and what I want to do.

So, take this opportunity because you've got another new day to start with. You might not have that day tomorrow. Accomplish and do as much as you can today to enrich your life. Give back to society and help those around you.

# Chapter 21
# Live Your Life with Passion

People talk about having a bucket list.

I would say, from the basics, look after yourself because your body is the only place you're ever going to live. So look after yourself mentally and physically. Do whatever it takes to keep yourself energized. Get enough sleep and eat the right foods. And be with people that you want to be with. Look for people who have similar goals, expectations, or themes in their lives. You want to attach yourself to those people.

Keep yourself strong mentally, physically, and emotionally so that you have the energy and capacity to be with people with similar goals instead of being with people who cause friction.

Next, have a list of things you want to accomplish. They could be significant, or they could be small.

Think about your legacy. When you're not here anymore, what will your legacy be? What are people going to say about you? Are you going to leave a lasting impression on people? Are you going to motivate the generation behind you?

We all have a purpose in life. For me, that purpose in life is to motivate and be an example.

You should hang around positive and energetic people who have similar goals. Join organizations you want to be part of, whether it's "Save the Whales" or "Hug a Tree." Whatever you are passionate about, do it and live it.

I would say don't go down your life's path because of your parents, siblings, or friends say, "Hey, you've got these talents. I think you should exploit them."

Follow your heart and your passions.

You might have a passion for journalism, a passion for being in the military, or a passion for playing football or basketball. You might think, "Hey, that won't be a career path that can put bread on the table, put gas in my tank, or pay the rent."

But something will evolve. It will make you a richer person mentally, physically, emotionally, and financially. In other words, if you are bored by the thought of being an accountant because your father said you are good with numbers and it is a safe career, then don't go to school to be an accountant.

Live your life by the passion in your heart and not by what you think the job opportunities will be down the road. Form your life based on your love and not necessarily what's available.

You'll know you're on track because you feel satisfied at the end of the day. You wake up in the morning with purpose. When you put your feet on the ground, you can say, "I will get out and accomplish these things today."

You have got a mental plan of what you want to do that day—versus lying in bed and hitting the snooze again and again and saying, "Oh man, I got to go to the office today."

Working on yourself mentally changes your energy. It gets your focus and purpose in life going in the right direction.

## Your Next Steps

You have read my stories. Hopefully, you have gained a new insight into how to create and lead teams. If you study these examples, you will become a better leader. You can use these stories as guideposts to help inspire you to become a better leader. More importantly, you will be a better person.

Thank you for taking this journey with me.

Please let me know how your journey continues as you build your teams and inspire your people.

## Questions to Educate, Empower, and Inspire

- What will you do differently right now?

# Epilogue

A big race was set for Veteran's Day, November 11, 2016, at Bagram Air Base just north of Kabul, Afghanistan. It was supposed to be the kickoff to a festive day to honor the heroes who served America.

It was not to be.

The runners showed up a little after 5:30 a.m. to prepare for the race, which was supposed to start at 6 a.m. before the desert heat became too oppressive.

Unbeknownst to them, a suicide bomber came into the crowd with his vest full of pellets, rocks, nails, and nasty stuff. He exploded himself and killed himself along with four Americans, injuring 14 others.

Pandemonium ensued. People were lying on the ground, bleeding out.

One man, Sergeant Kumar, ran to the blast site and began administering first aid to the soldiers. Sergeant Kumar was not a medic. However, like many soldiers deployed in a dangerous area, he was cross-trained as a Combat Life Saver to help others survive that important Golden Hour during emergency medical situations while they can then be evacuated and treated by medical professionals. He sprang into action because he knew people needed his help.

Coincidentally, I knew about the details of this story because my son, Adam, was Sergeant Kumar's supervisor.

Adam had planned to go to that event. However, he was on the night shift the night before and was too tired to go. He did not want to get up at 5 a.m.

He might have been killed or injured if he had gone to the run.

Soon after the attack, I flew into Bagram Airfield and Adam took me to the spot where the attack occurred. We saw a stop sign on the road that was close to the explosion. The stop sign was pockmarked with the shrapnel holes from the suicide bomber's improvised explosive device (IED). It is amazing more people were not hurt or killed.

I thought back to Vietnam when my team could have been air assaulted to the dangerous hill that got the other team killed.

I thought, "There for the grace of God go I."

My son and I both were granted God's good grace. And we live our lives to support and protect our American way of life and allow others to pursue the American Dream of "Life Liberty and the Pursuit of Happiness."

**Photo of father (Robert) and son (Adam) enjoying Christmas dinner together at Bagram Air Base, Afghanistan in 2016.**

# About the Author

**The author speaking at a Memorial Day event in Antioch, California**

Through his worldly travel experiences to over 75 countries, Robert (Bob) Hipwell, Ph.D., Brigadier General (Ret.) U.S. Army is inspired to give back to his community through his charity work with six Veterans Support Organizations (VSO) and by coaching, teaching, and mentoring corporate leaders.

He is an advocate for God, family, the military, veterans, and first responders. He speaks to veterans groups and corporations throughout the U.S. about teamwork, leadership, increasing the bottom line, as well as how to inspire yourself and your teams, and how to strengthen camaraderie.

He lives part-time outside Sacramento with his wife on a small ranch with two horses. He is the father of nine grown children and grandfather to 24 grandchildren. He enjoys mountain biking, hiking, golf, and skiing near his home in North Lake Tahoe, Nevada.

Bob can be reached at his web site:
www.GeneralRobertHipwell.com.

# Donations

A portion of the profits of this book will be donated to one or more of the following nonprofit organizations that I am personally involved with and support. I encourage you to look at them and potentially become involved in our overall mission of supporting our vulnerable Veteran Community, our military members, and our First Responders. Thank you!

## Placer Veterans Stand Down

https://placerveteransstanddown.org/
https://www.facebook.com/groups/532751717151021

## United States Volunteers - America

https://usv-a.org/
https://www.facebook.com/United-States-Volunteers-America-120972565183714

## The Honor Group

https://thehonorgroup.org/contact-the-honor-group/
https://www.facebook.com/HonorGroups

## Warriors for Life

https://www.victoryforveterans.org/

https://www.facebook.com/groups/1764479933863763

## Veterans Association of Real Estate Professionals (VAREP)

https://varep.net/

https://www.facebook.com/search/top?q=varep%20national

## Renew Restore Refit Community (R3C)

http://r3community.org/

# Acknowledgments

To Dan Janal, my co-author. You inspired me. You're the person I needed in my life to come along at this point. I've had this idea and thought about putting a book together for over ten years. I just haven't got off my ass enough to do it. But working with you is inspiring me.

The book sounds great and productive, and it will help many people. My ultimate goal is to get the book out there and help many people become inspirational leaders, both in the military and in the business community. If you'd like Dan to help you write your own book, you can read more about Dan at https://www.WriteYourBookInAFlash.com/

I would like to thank Doug Greene, who hosts the podcast, "WhatReallyMattersInterviews.com," for permission to use selected portions of his interview. You can listen to Doug's podcast here:

https://douggreene.net/wrm009-lessons-from-the-front-lines-of-war-interview-with-general-robert-hipwell/

This book is dedicated to those who change the lives of others by living as an example, inspiring and empowering others for greatness.

Some people I would like to make a special mention of who have inspired and empowered me with their enduring leadership and vision are General David Petraeus and General J.D. Thurman.

More people I would like to make a special mention of who have inspired and empowered me are Lieutenant General David H. Ohle, Lieutenant General William G. Webster, Major General Craig Bambrough, and Major General David L. Grange.

Some other very influential and inspirational people include WC Ballinger, Major General Rod Faulk, Major General Andy Juknelis, Colonel Scotty, Commander Mary C. Kelly, Major Charles A. Peak, Sergeant Major Richard Winkleman, Sergeant First Class Sammy L. Davis, Staff Sergeant Mike Vanning, and my sons who followed my example and served honorably and faithfully in the Army, Tim, Phil, Adam, Mathew, David, and Andrew.

And of course, I want to acknowledge my late father, Harold Robert Hipwell, who instilled basic values of right and wrong in me, taught me many of the ways of the world, and inspired me to follow in his footsteps to work hard and love your family. His favorite saying was, "Let's get organized here."

Have you inspired and empowered someone for greatness today?

If not, why not?

Made in the USA
Columbia, SC
29 September 2023

23572569R00109